Be still and cool in thy own mind and spirit from thy own thoughts, and then thou wilt feel the principle of God to turn thy mind to the Lord God… Do not look at the temptations, confusions, corruptions, but at the light that discovers them…and you will feel over them, to receive power to stand against them… For looking down at sin, and corruption, and distraction, you are swallowed up in it; but looking at the light that discovers them, you will see over them. That will give victory; and you will find grace and strength; and there is the first step of peace.

George Fox: Letter to Lady Claypole, 1658

Quakers stress the prayer of listening for divine guidance, a prayer that may not contain any words at all, even inwardly. Prayer can simply be the act or intention of being receptive to the Divine, not only to divine guidance, but to illumination, energy, healing, and the gradual process of union. When early Quakers wrote of their experiences in worship, they wrote of waiting in silence, emptying their minds of themselves and their own thoughts until they experienced a Presence among them.

Marcelle Martin (chapter 11)

Friends… noted a magnification of their spiritual experience in their Experimenting in Light groups, so they were aware that their experience was deepened and reinforced by their sharing: Experimenting led to their listening more, paying more attention to spiritual matters and deepening both daily spiritual practice and experience in meeting for worship.

Helen Meads (chapter 16)

Seeing, Hearing, Knowing

reflections on Experiment with Light

edited by John Lampen

WILLIAM SESSIONS LIMITED
YORK, ENGLAND
2008

ISBN 978-1-85072-372-1

We would like to thank the Sessions Book Trust, the Edith.M.Ellis Charitable Trust, the Robin Cullum Trust and several individual Friends for supporting the production of this book.

Reprinted 2010
Printed in Times New Roman
from Editor's Disk
by Sessions of York
The Ebor Press
York, England

CONTENTS

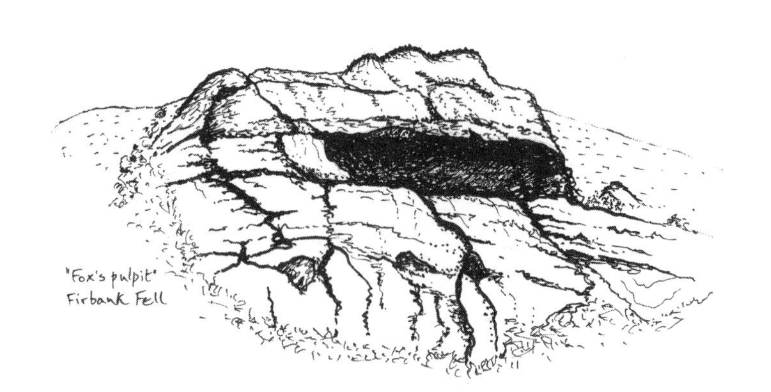
'Fox's pulpit'
Firbank Fell

George Fox's message on Firbank Fell

Rex Ambler

Three hundred and fifty five years ago, George Fox stood on a rock on Firbank Fell and preached to over one thousand people. It was the moment in which the Quaker movement really took off. From then on Fox had a band of men and women who would work alongside him to spread the message to the rest of England, and indeed, if possible, to the rest of the world. Fox had been waiting for this moment. He had had a vision when he stood on Pendle Hill some weeks before and, looking to the hill country in the north, "saw a great people to be gathered". He must have been anxious at that time, because so few people had responded to his message. It was a message of extraordinary power, he knew that, but few people had been willing or able to open themselves to it.

Now, in the western dales of Yorkshire and Westmorland, he found people who were ready, many hundreds of them. Moreover, they were already organized in groups, having "separated" themselves from the churches and started to look for an alternative. They also had "ministers" to look after them, like Francis Howgill and John Audland, but none of them had yet found what they were looking for. They called themselves "Seekers". They were expecting some new revelation from God, perhaps a new prophet or apostle who would bring them the truth, and something to live for and hope for. When they heard at the local fair, or by word of mouth, that George Fox was to be at Firbank Fell on the Sunday, they resolved to be there. Perhaps this was the man they had been waiting for. And Fox, when he met some of these people at the Sedbergh fair, knew that his dream of a "people to be gathered" was now to be realised.

They had wanted him, no doubt, to speak at the chapel on Firbank Fell. It was a surprising place for a chapel, in so remote a place; nothing now remains of it but a couple of gravestones. But there were many farms nearby, as there are now, though many more people then worked on them. The established church had realised that they needed a place to come to that was nearer than Sedbergh, down in the dale. There would be no hope of educating them otherwise. But the church abandoned the chapel during the civil war, which ended only in 1648, and it was taken up by the Seekers who needed a bigger place to meet in for their ever-increasing numbers. But Fox didn't go into the chapel. "I told them they must leave me to the

Lord's movings... I went to a brook and got me a little water".[1] He was not going to walk into their expectations. Instead, he waited for them to finish their service and come out onto the fell for their lunch—they were hoping, perhaps, for another service in the chapel later in the day, with or without Fox. When they were settled at their dinners, "I came and sat me down a-top of a rock, for the word of the Lord came to me I must go and set down upon the rock in the mountain even as Christ had done before. In the afternoon the people gathered about me with several Separate teachers, where it was judged there were above a thousand people; and all those several Separate teachers were convinced of God's everlasting Truth that day; amongst whom I declared freely and largely God's everlasting Truth and word of life about three hours".

Fox took them by surprise. This was something very new he had to say, and he had a new way of saying it, though somewhat reminiscent (what other model did he have?) of Jesus' own teaching in the Sermon on the Mount. "Many old people that went into the Chapel," he writes, "and looked out of the windows" —too frail, maybe, to sit out on the Fell— "thought it a strange thing to see a man to preach on a hill or mountain and not in their church (as they called it)." The effect was impressive. But the setting and style do not explain how at the end of that afternoon the teachers there "were convinced of God's everlasting truth that day". This had more to do with what Fox had to say.

It is difficult for us, 350 years later, to understand how Fox's preaching could have had such an effect. If we read his own summary of it in the Journal we get the impression he was giving them an interpretation of the Bible which must have been very familiar to them, and which may strike us as rather evangelical. And when we hear that the teachers were "convinced", we must assume that it was not quite what they were used to, but near enough to be convincing, that is, they were persuaded by his arguments. But if we read his account of his preaching on that day and read his tracts of the time we see very little argument in what Fox said. Listen to how he addressed them: "I was made to open to the people that…", "And so turning the people to the spirit of God, and from the darkness to the light…", etc. His challenge was more direct and personal. He was speaking to their condition, and therefore to their hearts. When they were "convinced" it meant they were deeply touched and affected by his words; but more than that, they were convinced of its truth and rightness by something deep in them, "the spirit of Truth", responding to what Fox said.

[1] These quotations are from Fox's own account of this day, 13 June 1652, in *The Journal of George Fox* (ed. John Nickalls, Religious Society of Friends, 1975) pages 108-109

But Fox was down to earth as well. He started his talk by referring, literally, to the ground on which they were standing. "I was made to open to the people that the steeplehouse and that ground on which it stood were no more holy than that mountain, and those temples and 'dreadful houses of God' (as they called them) were not set up by the command of God nor Christ". They had come to the chapel because they thought it was the "house of God", so Fox addresses their condition: they are living under an illusion. The building, which had been put up by humans after all, was no more holy than the mountain where they were standing now, out in the open. (That was how Christ had taught, and Fox had felt "moved" to do the same.) The sacred could not be found in humanly constructed things. It was in their hearts, first of all, if they could find a way in. So he concluded his three-hour "sermon" by "turning the people to the spirit of God, and from the darkness to the light". Note the language that he used here: he "turned" them around to face the light. They had been looking outwards, to buildings, priests, hoped-for prophets in the mistaken belief that these could help them and make them whole. That was their "darkness", their delusion.

It is often said that when Fox spoke on Firbank Fell the expectations of the Seekers were met perfectly in Fox himself, that the Quaker movement began precisely with the meeting between these two. But you can see that this was not really the case. There was a great meeting here, certainly, but Fox had first to disappoint them and break their expectations: he refused to go into their chapel, he brought them out on a mountain, and he refused to be their teacher, he pointed them instead to the teacher they had within them. This would be a huge turn around for the Seekers, and they would need to be seriously "convinced" if they were now to abandon the belief system which they still held on to.

So Fox spends much of his time in the sermon going over this belief system, which had kept them, and many other people, in the dark. They had believed, to begin with, that the truth had been revealed in a book, the Bible, and that ministers and priests had been appointed to interpret this truth to them and impart the benefits of it through sacraments like baptism and eucharist. These special people were, to use the language of the Bible, their "bishops", "shepherds" and "prophets". But thinking in this way puts truth and grace and life outside them, as something they have to imbibe. Fox comes close to saying they have to buy it from the priests(!), because part of the system was the payment of tithes, one tenth of all their income, for the maintenance of the priests. The priests, meanwhile, "make a trade of their words (the apostles' words) and have put them into chapter and verse", which then need to be interpreted (by the priests of course). This is not only deceitful, he implies, it is grossly unjust and oppressive.

All this is evident from the fact that Christ had come, originally, to "end" that system of belief and practice, and to lead people into a quite different way of life, in which they could "learn from Christ" themselves. "But Christ was come, who ended the temple, and the priests, and the tithes, and Christ said 'Learn of me'". So, Fox is showing them, the system, which idolises Christ, is a blatant contradiction. It says one thing and does another. In fact it is exalting the image of Christ only to smother his message. The so-called followers of Christ have therefore reverted to the system that Christ had come to abolish.

How then can they recover the power and truth that Christ had revealed? Not by studying the scriptures or attending church services, neither of which could break the spell. They would understand the scriptures well, and worship God well, only when they had first come to the spiritual teacher within themselves, "that with the spirit of Truth they might be led into all the Truth of the prophets', Christ's and the apostles' words."

But how do they do that? Fox doesn't answer that question in his summary of his speech, but he does elsewhere.[2] They come to the "spirit of Truth" by looking for signs of disturbance in themselves: twitches of conscience, feelings of oppression, anxiety about themselves. They were then to look at the situation that those feelings referred to, and to let the reality of it be opened to them. They had to be still and silent for this to happen, to adopt an attitude of openness and expectancy, otherwise their own thoughts and fears would take over. If they were open, however, they would begin to see things they had never seen before. The spirit deep within them would shed light on what was going on in their life, what they were doing or not doing, and why. It would show them the truth about themselves. If they accepted the truth revealed, however difficult, they would see everything else more clearly, not least how they could now live their lives more freely and fully. The truth would free them from their dependence on authorities and enable them to trust their own inner resources. It would free them from fear of others (and fear of life) and enable them to love one another and bond with one another. Out of this a true, viable community would emerge, which would give them all the support they needed. This would be a true "church", the Christ within them would be a real "teacher and shepherd", and their own bodies would be "temples of God and of Christ".

That is how Fox "turned the people from the darkness to the light", and when many were "convinced that day", he knew that it was the light within them that had really done the work.

[2] I am drawing, in what follows, on *The Journal of George Fox* especially two letters on pp. 142f, 346-8; and my own anthology of Fox, *Truth of the Heart* (Quaker Books, 2007), sections 1:1, 31, 34, 40, 41, 61, 69, 82, 91; 2:1,18,79,81.

Longing for the Light

Anne Hosking

The Experiment with Light grew out of personal experience, tested and found true, then shared with others, and again tested and found true. Rex Ambler's many years' study of early Quaker theology and George Fox's writings in particular had showed him a spiritual discipline. However, it was so commonly practised among early Friends it was taken for granted. This spiritual discipline was not set out in steps, it was learned by association and by doing, rather than taught as a method: one has to hunt through the writings to find the clues. At Yearly Meeting 1997 in Aberystwyth, Rex shared his discovery with two members of the Quaker Retreat Group, who promptly organized two gatherings which overflowed with Friends eager to make the experiment too. Afterwards, he had more invitations to meetings than he could cope with. Small groups caught the idea and began spontaneously to meet. It was time to pass on his insights and the meditations he had developed to others. Some months later, two dozen Friends met at Glenthorne, the Quaker conference centre in the English Lake District.[1]

I glimpsed a little of what drew us together for the week, and some of the questions in our hearts. There were people in paid and unpaid work, in different family situations, those involved in healing the wounds of society and tackling the causes, teachers and a number of counsellors or psychotherapists. Are they doing the right thing? Where is the strength they need? Some have been searching through different faith communities, and having reached Friends want to find out about the root-experience of Quakers. Did they seek a deeper understanding of what it is to be truly human, to see something so central one could call it "that of God" in the other? A closer link between the spiritual and the everyday?

And me? I had many reasons, but what had bothered me most was a recent comment from an old friend, now a bishop. He asked me what I was doing these days, I replied that I was involved in retreats among Quakers, and he said "But what have Quakers to …" and then stopped himself in embarrassment. What have Quakers to offer? That was indeed the question before us at Glenthorne.

We do have our meetings for worship, but it can be quite hard for a newcomer to know what to do, how the worship works. Friends seem reluctant to explain; the eager enquirer has to turn detective, alert to small clues in behaviour or

[1] The participants' own words, taken from my verbatim notes, formed the basis of a report for the British weekly Quaker journal, *The Friend*, on which this chapter draws.

conversation that suggest the power behind our witness and service. Sometimes our lives speak in rather garbled language.

Though retreats and quiet days are increasingly popular among Friends, the work, the rhythm and focus of these events are generally borrowed from the Ignatian exercises, Benedictine *lectio divina*, Celtic ritual, Buddhist mindfulness. Friends are open to the insights and grateful for all these gifts from other traditions, but we must surely have something that is not secondhand, our own particular gift or the divine *charism* to which we are called. After all, early Quakers seemed to have a strong spiritual life, something very powerful going on inside them that changed lives and that could change society. It was authentic, original, not copied. What was it? I wanted that transforming joy that early Quakers were willing to pay for with their lives. What was their discipline of seeking—and more important, of finding?

Did the early Quakers really practise a systematic meditation? What did it mean? Did it work? Would it make a difference in our lives? Was the experiment with light truly Fox, or just Rex? We would have to do the experiment ourselves.

A Spiritual Hunger

The phrase "spiritual hunger" is used so often to describe how Friends are now, but what might it mean? I meet many Friends who are well-nourished in their meetings, but I also meet many who are disappointed. I hear them say things like "I wanted to talk about bringing up our children in a Quakerly way, and they suggested I write to Friends House for a book". "I offered a prayer in ministry, and afterwards someone asked if I was all right". "I ministered about … [insert any powerful word]… and I was told that was not Quakerly, it upset them". "I needed help in discerning what to do about… but there never seemed time to talk to anyone." It is not that anyone wishes to be obtuse or resistant to spiritual questions, and certainly everyone bemoans the pressure of Quaker business—or is that an escape from Something? Do we deal with what is urgent before what is important?

Nonetheless, our hunger is actually a sign of healing, for those who are really sick lack hunger: they lose their sense of taste and smell, they lose their appetites. Those who are starving conserve their energy, they stay still and take no risks. There are many negative statements in modern Quakerism—we are not this, we do not do that, we would not believe something else. To recent "refugees" from other churches or faiths Quakerism may be valued chiefly for those aspects that are not whatever they have rejected! Some see a rabid pluralism, an unbounded relativism, an abandonment, even a despair that we cannot share anything but are isolated individuals, with no common language. Many have called present day Quakerism a pick'n'mix faith. Gerald Priestland said that we are not being fed much in meeting, so we bring our own packed lunches.[2] Are we offering junk food?

Where is the Quaker reality? What is the fundamental experience that we are supposed to be about? The ground of our faith is not doctrinal, not credal, but experiential—yes, but what is that experience? Is there an experience in common? What makes us Friends together?

There was a light, a fire, a renewal among early Quakers, such that the movement swept the country and within a very few years about one in 130 of the population were counted as Quakers. Was there a hope—or risk—of real change in our human society? The king and government were forced to repress the early Friends. Though there is no record of these early Quakers recanting, or meeting in secret, they did modify that early faith in defence: by the end of the seventeenth century they had become respectable. And as they regularized their structure and their worship, the memory of those ten years or so was softened and their numbers diminished. Moderation, reason and safety reigned.

Where is the light now, the fire of early Friends, their spirit of renewal that revolutionised religious thinking over 350 years ago? We are seekers, but are we looking for the right things, in the right places, in the right way? Are we finding and, having found, are we proclaiming?

We listened to the words of hunger and rephrased them as a longing for light. So many of us live in a city and work indoors. I remember childhood summers in Latin America, the intense reds of flowers, the many browns of skin and the black grains of volcanic sand, when I could see so clearly my eyes hurt. In the short days of the northern European winter, colours are dulled and we see people in dark clothes, expressionless faces, scurrying by. We can sense people losing energy and a sense of purpose.

It is not surprising that such longing for clarity and intensity of colour has a counterpart in a yearning for light, and that light offers a particularly helpful way of exploring the divine. For George Fox *Light* (with a capital L) was one of the richest symbols for or manifestations of God. In contrast, the declaration that "There is that of God in everyone", which is so popular it has become credal in practice among late 20th and 21st century Quakers, occurred only five

[2] Gerald Priestland: *Reasonable Uncertainty* (Quaker Home Service, 1982) p.8

times in his *Journal*. The shorter phrase "that of God" was vastly outnumbered by Light, Light of Christ, Power of the Lord, and other phrases.[3]

We need courage to face the Light. George Fox was well aware of what leads to obtuseness. He wrote of "the veiled mind" and warned Friends "give not way to the lazy, dreaming mind". [4] The Light is here, now, available in each one of us, in our hearts, facing us now, but we ignore it, or minimize it, or fear what it may show us. We need courage and the companionship and support of others, if we are to face the Light.

The courage needed in the first instance is not so much physical as moral. The physical courage may indeed be needed when we try to live and work according to the Light. The Light does not deal in illusion or self-delusion, and there is no room for cheap comfort. Comfort—in the root sense of the word, "strengthening, empowering, fortifying with others"—is promised, and that is a true promise, in my experience, worth the effort, but the effort and the courage have to come first. Thank God for Friends.

Experimenting With Light

We were members of at least six Yearly Meetings, with as many mother tongues, though we used mostly English at Glenthorne. We had different personalities, so we heard and spoke with different understandings. We came from a variety of backgrounds, and used different terminology—Buddhist, Jungian, New Age, Christian of different kinds, and more—but it was the seventeenth century English of George Fox that gave us most work.

Fox's images and references are strongly Biblical: those who have little acquaintance with the Bible could have difficulty even getting started. Some whose own earlier experience of Christianity was oppressive felt that Fox, too, was trying to prescribe and ensure conformity. His language is outmoded—can't we just do the meditation in contemporary words, and bypass Fox? His sentences were often imperative in grammatical form—he sounded so dogmatic and authoritarian!

Fox used many words for the divine, *God, Christ within, Seed, Light* and *Power* being the most common, perhaps. As we explored aspects of the divine, we began to recognize typical ways of relating to this holy mystery. Clarifying

[3] Joseph Pickvance: *A Reader's Companion to George Fox's Journal* (Quaker Home Service, 1989) p.126

[4] Rex Ambler: *Truth of the Heart* (Quaker Books, 2007). The quotations I give from George Fox are taken from this collection, using Rex's modern rendering.

words was how we started. A glossary is an important part of *Truth of the Heart,* the anthology Rex compiled of Fox's writings, setting out his experiment. Rex had come to discern Fox's method of meditation through a study of his writings, an academic path, which we followed too that week. What Rex had found was simple, specific, relevant, precise, beautiful—it was so clear. This, it seemed, was how Friends attended to the Light. Rex had not heard Quakers speaking like this since. If he followed Fox, tried out the light, what would he discover?

Seed indicates the potential, the possibility of growth (but also the character of that person or soul, for each seed is of its kind), "the seed of God" within. And after the seed grows, there is harvest. "Threshing" has been rediscovered among Friends in recent years—we say that we thresh an issue, discussing all aspects without pressure or limit, before we try to make a decision. In our worship that week, however, we learned that it is we ourselves, not the issue, who are threshed, "chaff without thee, the chaff within…" . Then we are winnowed by sacred winds, the chaff blown away, the kernels remaining.

Light, we were to discover, is both within and without, and has the characteristic of searching, showing, lightening (as in enlightening). It can be comforting and warm, but often it has fierce power, like a laser, or a flash of lightning. Margaret Fell had warned that "the Light will rip you open", a phrase that echoed during the week as we faced the Light with courage.[5] Indeed, declared Fox, the Light "will let thee see thy heart", it "shows you when you do wrong", "it will reprove you", and yes, it hurts to see these things. But "if you love this light it will teach you", "it will lead you into the way of peace". Yes, there is healing and hope too.

Some of us had queried the emphasis on light, and we were aware that the metaphor of light can be used in a hurtful way, as if darkness is evil. We worried that light versus dark might be understood as a racist contrast. However, Light was a word that Fox used for life-changing experience. We had to follow his steps until we understood his meaning for ourselves, only then would we be free to discard the word. We used the word with humility. We were conscious of the goodness of darkness, where the seed grows safely, where labour and birth so often take place, where one rests and dreams, and were grateful for the dark.

God underwent the same process. We had to be tender of the various words that, for each individual, had become a treasured expression of Something that is, in essence, inexpressible. After a couple of days of using alternative words and attempts at periphrasis, we seemed to settle on Fox's favourite Light, Seed,

[5] Hugh Barbour: *Margaret Fell Speaking*, (Pendle Hill Pamphlet 206, 1976) p.24

God, Power. These were the most useful tools while exploring his "experiment", but used with caution.

Was there a linguistic tension, even a hostility, between us now and Friends then? Did we need to forgive the seventeenth century, I wondered?

Take ***experiment*** itself: at the turn of the 20th century it has a mostly scientific meaning—to try something out, to see what happens, usually with a hypothesis to test, some result you are aiming it. Experimenting is seen as such a "good thing" it can even be used to justify risky behaviour such as drug-taking or dangerous sports, or promoting individual rights and pleasures over community responsibilities and duties.

Though Fox used the word to refer to scientific testing, he laid more emphasis on experiment meaning direct experience, reality. He *knew* that when we open ourselves to God, God is there, but he also knew that we have to do that knowing for ourselves. He had confidence in the outcome of the experiment, he had no doubt what we would find. His task was to encourage us to dare the experiment, and it is precisely because the experiment with Light is experiential that it is Quakerly, Christian and universal. There is a basic human awareness of the Light in each one of us, in each person. It is Christian, too, for Fox identified that inward Light with the Christ that is within Jesus and within us. What we learn, and how we live it out in our lives will be *particular* (another Foxian word), but it starts from the universality of direct experience.

Universal: I saw that when we trusted this universality, we could deal better with the specificity of Fox's language—the symbols he used, the seventeenth century vocabulary and grammar. There was, however, a tension among us. For example, Friends belong to a meeting, we do not follow a guru or believe in a book. A meeting is where together we turn to the Light, in all our individuality. For some of us, the fact that philosophers, theologians, mystics, psychologists and prophets of other traditions offered similar insights and process seemed to diminish the Quaker gift. Nothing special, it's all the same, really. For others, this similarity confirmed that Fox had something authentic and *true* (yet another Foxian term), and it was worth finding out more. How could we hold in unity the particular and the universal? We recognized with gratitude a truth offered, with humility:

> *We are a particular people, participating in the universal, but there is an integrity in the Quaker way, such that it would be a diminishment of the universal if we were to discard or damage what we have found to be true.*

We all have a portion, but only a portion, of the Light. Thus we need each other, whether in the context of Friends, society as a whole, or as churches and faiths, to achieve spiritual wholeness.

That of God, we learnt, was almost always misquoted and misunderstood. When you read Fox out loud (he dictated almost all his epistles and his journals), you can hear the eloquence and urgency, words tumbling out with eagerness and force, sentences that do not always end the way you expect. "That of God" was shorthand for "that of God within you which …", which shows you reality, which teaches you, which challenges. It should not be equated with "something good", suggesting that all people are really good and nice, if only we cared enough. "That of God" like the Seed is a potential, an ability, a spark of God in each of us that can grow and be nurtured, that can enlighten us, but that growth is not inevitable.

Another word is ***Truth***, not just truths, facts, but something that seems like another understanding of the divine. Truth is always practical, to be lived, for "there are too many talkers, and few walkers in Christ". The Truth shows recognizable facts about ourselves, e.g. lust, drunkenness, violence. Truth leads us to be whole people, without deluding ourselves, without hypocrisy—as moderns would say, with integrity—or as Fox said, "being single before the Lord." We need to tread and trample all deceit under foot in ourselves… then "things may be spoken in nakedness of heart one unto another".

Each has a measure of the Light, enough, and what is right for that person, but partial—hence our need for each other, so each measure of the Light complements the other. One could say this also of cultures, faiths and even meetings—each has a measure of the Light, we are responsible for our own measure, and it is ours to respect and develop, but also we should know that our Light complements and enhances the Light of others.

The Light shows us the Truth that we need to know, each one of us in our own situation. When we see truly, then we can know what we must do next.

Consequence: When we are open to "the wisdom of God and the life of God in ourselves", we will "do rightly, justly, truly, holy, equally to all people…" Quakers are not the only people to see a unity in faith and works, of course. Nonetheless, prayer as Friends understand it is completed in service, or rather the prayer and the service are one. Unless we care, witness and serve, we cannot say we have a spiritual life.

Exploring these words and concepts had taken us closer to George Fox, ready to follow him in a step by step experiment in Quaker meditation. We had heard enough from Rex and from others who have been practising this meditation, we were ready to be challenged and changed. Would it work?

A Meditation on Light

George Fox tried to show people a way of meditation that has no form, that is about abandoning all forms, all outward signposts, all guidelines, so that in the end there is no meditation. And in that meditation, the Light will come, showing you what you need to see. The process can't be taught, but it can be learnt.

It is so simple: you look into your conscience, your self, and let the Light show you the truth about your own life. When you see that truth, you will also see what you have to do and be. And how do you gain access to this Light? Stand still… turn to the light… wait… in silence… wait. The steps could be set out like this:

> First you stop whatever you are doing or thinking—"Be still and cool in thy own mind and spirit from thy own thoughts." It helps to be still in the body, too.
>
> Then, stay there, do not DO anything. You will "feel the principle of God turn thy mind to the Lord God".
>
> Stay in the Light—you do not need to tell the Light what to do, or why you are there, or engage in conversation with the Light, you just wait.

That's it. When you wait in the Light, the Light shows you whatever you need to see. It will change you, rebuke you, heal you, give you life—whatever is right for you. Really, there is no "meditation", no technique or process. Like meeting for worship, there is no form, you just do it. Indeed, there were times when I could see no difference between the meditation and meeting for worship, and other times when I saw the need for a particular guide, to be discarded in time.

Fox does not describe this systematically, but it is all in his writings, and those of other very early Quakers. You need to look for it, though it is easy to find, for example by tracing all references to Light in *Quaker Faith & Practice*, or reading John Lampen's *Wait in the Light.*[6] Fox was not teaching a method of meditation, rather he was directing people to God, to the Light within themselves. He was showing them how to recognize it, he was urging them to trust it, but most of all he was showing in his own life and attitude that the Light was trustworthy and effective. What followed once you turned to the Light was up to you and the Light, it would be particular to you.

Rex's explanation illuminated something that had bothered me for years. Time after time in Fox's writings, in journals, in early accounts of people ministering

[6] John Lampen: *Wait in the Light: the spirituality of George Fox* (Quaker Home Service, 1981)

in meetings, Friends wrote of telling their listeners to turn to "Christ who was within and would teach them". I expected these sentences to continue "and what he taught them was…". We always seemed to be left hanging in the air. I was expecting Fox to interpret Christ's teaching, to summarise it for me, to set it out clearly, and he did not. I began to learn something of the character of the Light. The Truth is there, you don't have to go on a long journey. The Light does not show you other things, people, but yourself. The Light will show you your own condition, "let the Light search us thoroughly".

There's nothing to do, no envisioning, no physical exercises, or symbolic stages—just turn round, see, stand still. Fox describes what will happen next, in consequence: "then power (i.e. the ability to cope with what the Light shows) comes, then content comes, and peace". We were to trust the Light.

That was because Fox had total trust in your inward teacher—he did not need to do any interpreting, his job was to lead you to that inward teacher, to get you to turn to the Light. Fox would pull back at that point, leave you responsible for what you would then see in the Light. "Don't gad abroad", he said. There is no need to wander round the religious world, projecting your wants and imaginings. The Truth is within you, here, now, ready, available.

We can help each other by the way we "answer that of God" in one another—we do not just react. We certainly do not give a solution to a question. "Answer" in Fox's usage is active, even interactive. I thought of the way we react to a baby's babbling—we respond to the baby, we imitate the noises, the baby babbles back, we confirm the sounds, and so the baby learns to speak. The answering evokes, calls out something from the other.

Rex found in his reading of Fox that this lesson applies to the individual, to groups, and to the "world" and that how to be open to that Light was a process that we as individuals, as groups and meetings—and, maybe, the world—can engage in. It had functioned like a DIY therapy for him, giving a clarity that was not instant or comprehensive, but developing. He gained over time the insight and the tranquil trust he needed to start dealing with certain problems. That encouraged us to risk the experiment ourselves.

We need, however, to remember Margaret Fell's experience, that "the Light will rip you open". It can be painful, shaming or upsetting before it becomes healing and transforming. Jacob only knew he had been blessed, after he was wounded in the struggle with the angel. When I invited people to experiment I therefore put the "meditation" early in the day, thus allowing time for this demanding work of waiting in the Light, and made sure there was support if needed. I used the historical discussion after (rather than before), as the occasion for shared reflection. Others have set up small groups that meet at intervals over a long period. The group offers both a disciplined framework and loving support. This, of course, is precisely what meetings are for, with their eldership and oversight. An experiment with Light is not a one-off exercise or event. It is a practice and a way of living in the Spirit.

As we completed our time together at Glenthorne, we reviewed our questions. There is a technique of meditation, a process of experiment with Light? It works? And can anyone learn it and use it too? Yes, we agreed, and it works, and you can become transformed.

The paradox is that you can learn it, but no, you cannot be taught it, for it is actually a non-technique. It is like meeting for worship, where trying too hard defeats the stillness. The process sketched above is not like the steps of a highly structured meditation, such as are found in the dozens of best-selling books. There can never be *A Little Book of Experimenting with Light*! You catch the trust and courage from someone else, or from your own emptying. This is the paradox, setting up a way of meditation that has no form, that is about abandoning all forms, all outward signposts, all guidelines, so that in the end there is no meditation—just wait in the Light.

An Epistle

Love and Light to Friends everywhere from the Experiment with Light gathering at Glenthorne, Grasmere, 1-5 November 2004.

The Experiment with Light aims at connecting us with the Divine and at enabling us to find the truth of which George Fox said: "This I knew experimentally". Many of us have experienced the Light as a transforming power in our individual lives and in our relationships with others. It challenges us to face the reality about ourselves and the world and encourages us to live more mindfully and more adventurously. Our lives can become ongoing experimentations with Light.

The Light, as Fox put it, shows us all that is out of the Light, and such insights into the darker sides of ourselves or the world can be painful and challenging. We were reminded of how important it is not to shy away from such revelations. When we have faith in the process, the Light will show us a way out of the darkness and guide us into spiritual renewal.

The Experiment with Light must not be misunderstood as a form of therapy. It is a rediscovery of a spiritual process with which early Friends were familiar, enriched by the diversity of our present day culture. It is not a particular meditation, but has developed different forms in the few years of its existence.

It has been suggested to us that the Religious Society of Friends as a whole is an Experiment with Light or, to use the words of William Penn, "a spiritual experiment upon the soul". We are struggling to find ways of making our practice more widely known and better understood. We realize that words are inadequate to capture our experience and may lead to conflict and misunderstandings. Words are mere vehicles to convey what we know in our hearts and what is ultimately beyond words. This is what the Experiment teaches us.

We are convinced that the Experiment with Light should not be the special interest of a minority, as it is a practice that could immensely enrich the life of our Meetings. We invite all Friends who have not yet done so to share this treasure with us by embarking on the Experiment yourselves. May you be blessed with the same sense of healing and joy that we have found, and may we all grow together in listening more attentively to the promptings of love and truth in our hearts.

A Quaker Jewel

John M Daly

I first learned about the Experiment with Light in 2003 from a workshop run by John and Diana Lampen at the Quaker Settlement in Wanganui, New Zealand, although I had already done some homework beforehand by reading Rex Ambler's two books, *Truth of the Heart* and *Light to Live By*. What follows is my personal view of the Experiment, not a group view or a Meeting view. I have had feedback from the others with whom I have done the Experiment and revised my account in the light of their comments but it remains an account of my personal experience.

I think I was predisposed towards Experiment with Light by two earlier experiences. Firstly I had attended a Focusing workshop run by an inspiring Canadian teacher, Nada Lou, in 2002. The process of focusing is described in Eugene Gendlin's book *Focusing*.[1] I found this workshop an amazing experience, where I first got a real "felt sense"—a very graphic one, of hands throttling me—and of release when I found the "handle" or way to put the "felt sense" into words.[2] This two-day workshop gave me a major insight about the way I approach the world, which still resonates in my life even five years later. Secondly, I was already a committed meditator, beginning in 1993 and meditating at least 20 minutes morning and evening most days. I use both Loving Kindness meditation[3] and Breath Counting. These are now part of my core practice and I can't imagine that I will voluntarily stop doing these. Also, for the last three years I have been doing 20 minutes writing practice most mornings[4]. These practices give me part of the perspective with which I see the Experiment. From the writing practice I have accumulated many pages of notes about my experiences with it.

I found the whole Wanganui workshop a very moving experience and was very grateful for the afternoon "free times" to recover—I think otherwise it might have been just too much to take. I didn't feel that I had any major insights or experiences of a "felt sense" during the workshop itself. Other people in my home group (another really valuable feature of the workshop format) did have real "aha!" moments and I found the others in the group really supportive of my fumbling attempts to put my experiences into words.

1 Eugene Gendlin: *Focusing* (Bantam Books, 1981)
2 see page 38
3 Stephen Levine, *Healing into Life and Death* (Gateway, 1989)
4 Julia Cameron, *The Artist's Way* (Pan, 1997)

Paradoxically my own "aha" moment came not in the workshop but during a quiet day that Diana facilitated at the end of the workshop. I have now forgotten the theme for the quiet day, but still vividly remember someone in a Meeting for Worship telling of their vision of Jesus preaching the "good news" by the lakeside. Somehow I "knew" that I couldn't say this for myself—experientially—though I think the person giving the ministry did so know it for herself. This is something I'm still struggling with, having been brought up as an Anglican, spending thirty years or so as an "on paper" Buddhist, and ten years as a "Quaker". Now I am re-exploring my childhood path to the teaching of Jesus, while trying to lay aside some of the later accretions of Christianity. Paradoxically, the practice has recently been a great support to me while working though the process of leaving the Quaker Meeting here.

Starting a Light Group for Christchurch Monthly Meeting

The two of us from Christchurch who had attended the Wanganui workshop decided that we would offer the Meeting the chance to try the Experiment for themselves. We decided to run a series of evening sessions to try and pass on the background information that John and Diana had given us in the workshop and then end with an experience of the process itself. This was with some trepidation on my part, as I felt I would be trying to teach something I had not had time to practise for myself first. I think we had four evening sessions before the one where we put on the tape (Rex Ambler's tape with the longer introductions). Unfortunately quite a few of the people who had come along initially had already decided it was not for them before we got to the process itself, so they never actually tasted the Experiment themselves.

We ended up as a core group of only three people, so I suppose that the Light Group hasn't has a great effect on the Monthly Meeting as a whole. Over the four years, a few extra people have joined in occasionally but only the core group has continued. We have generally met once a fortnight, which we've seen as a compromise between the time constraints of busy lives and a desire for continuity of practice.

Those of us who have persevered have found the Light Group a very valuable experience. Otherwise we would not have continued with it for so long. Right from the beginning we have regularly had a period of Creative Listening after the practice itself. The whole process takes between seventy-five and ninety minutes. This gives us the opportunity, though definitely not the obligation, to share some or all of our experiences with the Experiment. I have found this one of the most helpful parts of the process, as it has given me a chance to try and put my experiences into words and thus help to clarify it and give them a context.

One modification suggested by one of the other group members, is that we introduced a five minute period of silence to settle down from our busy days, before we start the tape. I have now incorporated this opening silence when making new copies of the meditation disc. I try to decide beforehand on the area I would like to bring into the Light. I know this is not in the original instructions and could be seen as an attempt to control the process but I have found it helpful. Otherwise I find that I can spend a large part of the meditation itself trying to decide between competing problems.

One of the other members of the Light Group has commented to me about how often, when we have shared our experiences that they turned out to reflect, echo or amplify those of the other people in the group. It was almost as though there was somehow a shared component in our apparently separate meditations.

At present we have been in recess for a few months but we are hoping to resume shortly. This break has been on account of pressure of other commitments, but it has also given us a chance to reassess the role that Experiment with Light fills in our lives.

A Distance Learning Light Group

As well as the small Light Group within the Christchurch Monthly Meeting I have taken part in an experiment with a "distance learning" model. One of the other people who attended the initial Wanganui workshop also came from the South Island but she was unable to find anyone in her MM to join her in setting up a Light Group. So we agreed to try out a different model. We agreed by e-mail on times when we would both do the practice and then one of us would phone the other, turn and turn about, to talk about our experiences.

We have both found that it worked better than we had expected; I know I did, and that we have become closer friends through this process. We have mostly tried to limit phone calls to an hour or less and made use of capped off-peak phone charges so that the cost has not been an issue, at least not for me. We have probably met face to face perhaps half a dozen times over the four years since we started and have tried to fit in a "normal" Experiment with Light session on these occasions.

Some surprises along the way

I think one of the things that amazes me most is how often the Experiment resulted in my seeing (over and over) that what I needed most was to let go of ideas, of ways of thinking: to let go of things that were already all too firmly embedded in my mind. Saying this makes the Experiment sound rather negative, but in fact the process of letting go of so many burdens that I hadn't known I was carrying, was a relief at a very profound level. Even letting go of the idea that the Light Group had to be successful for other people as well as for me (whatever "being successful" might mean) in order for me to feel comfortable with it, was for me quite a major achievement. Also learning to relax into the Light, even occasionally, rather than treating it as one more thing "I" had to do well. For a dyed-in-the-wool academic, learning that it's okay, even sometimes, not to know the answer was a major step—even learning that not all the answers to important questions are in books, to the extent that sometimes now I wonder if any of them are.

Another thing that has surprised me in retrospect is how often my most moving experiences of the Experiment involved my coming up with spontaneous prayers. For someone brought up with the idea that prayers were things written in books (by other people), this was truly revolutionary.

My overall impressions of the Practice

In my less reverent moments I think of Experiment with Light as a portable DIY Meeting for Worship, especially when I'm doing it on my own. The periodic comments by Rex Ambler or Diana Lampen on the tape or CD serve to bring me back to the present and sometimes to strike sparks from my wayward mind, just as ministry may do in a "normal" Meeting for Worship. For those of us whose names are not Teresa of Avila or Julian of Norwich, the results and benefits of using the Experiment may be just as hard to define as those of any other form of meditation. I may spend the actual time of meditation trying to decide which of my many pressing problems to focus on, or even trying to rewrite the wording of the meditation in my head, and feel at the end of the session that I have not achieved anything helpful at all. But then suddenly, while I'm shaving or pulling up weeds in the garden, the cluster bomb dropped by Experiment with Light explodes and there is a hole in the previously forbidding wall which had enclosed me, or I may see that my favourite enemy, the person I love to hate the most, has these endearing good points, which I had somehow overlooked before. All of a sudden, the world looks a less forbidding place, becomes a more do-able enterprise than I had feared it was. Those people who don't have a background experience in depression may find these particular examples more difficult to relate to.

Also the outcome of a session often only becomes clear (in my experience anyway), during a time of sharing after the practice itself has ended. When we share our distractions, our inability to settle, our experiences, by putting them into words, perhaps for the first time ever, we may suddenly find that perhaps we are not as alone on our journeys as we had supposed. I know that for me the EwL practice has provided a sort of link between meditation, which often seems rather self- orientated, and the "real world". In the end, as with other forms of meditation, I think the important thing is to practice it, rather than spending time wondering about how and why it works. I for one am very grateful that I have had the chance to experience its working.

This We Can Say

Bronwen and John Gray

We have had the privilege of being part of an Experiment with Light group for about eight years now. The journey has been like the path of a river—sometimes straight, at other times meandering, sometimes smooth, at other times filled with rapids. But what has been constant is the movement; rarely have we felt that we are standing still.

Bronwen says:

Although the Experiment with Light process is based on verbal questioning, the responses to these questions always come to me in the form of images. So after our forty minutes or so going through the steps, invariably I get out paper, paint, glue, scissors—whatever I need to recreate the image that I have been shown. I've included two such images in this chapter.

One of the earliest images was of a figure—presumably me—standing on top of a tall block of flats, speaking into a megaphone. I was shouting about the Experiment with Light, which was for me a new and exciting discovery. Right from the beginning of my encounter with this process I felt it would be important for me, and could be for many others. It came as no surprise, then, that some years later John and I found ourselves facilitating Experiment with Light sessions for other Friends.

Another memorable image came to me when I was seeking discernment about a job application. I asked some fairly direct questions, along the lines of, 'Is this the job for me?' The 'answer' came in the image of a vase containing dead flowers. The meaning was clear: there is no life in this job. In some ways the answer was disappointing, but I knew it was right and there was no question of my taking that job.

A constant theme has been that of needing time for spiritual nurture. Since starting the Experiment we have had two children, and I have found that my time for personal reflection has become more limited. My need for inner calm and nurture has not gone away, so the recurring images on this theme come as no great surprise. I regularly see an image of a well, with myself sitting at the top, needing desperately to sink to the bottom of the well and drink the water. Another image is of a tree reaching deep down to its roots for nourishment, as in the image shown. So Experiment with Light can serve as a timely reminder of what I should already be aware of, but all too often neglect.

Another regular image is that of the Light itself. I sometimes see a bright ball shape within myself, and on several occasions have tried to portray this—with an outline of myself with a white mass of light inside me. On one occasion I saw myself as a mountain surrounded by light. These are very empowering images; they remind me that the Light really is there, and if only I listen I will discover what I need to know.

There have been times when I've had no helpful image. While this can be disappointing, I generally find that this tells me something that I need to acknowledge. Either I am too tired, or simply not centred enough to properly engage. Time is never wasted, though, as I find the structure of our Experiment with Light evenings very helpful. We have a chance to share with the group what has happened in our lives since we last met, then after the practice itself we have about 20 minutes of personal reflection. In the busyness of our life with jobs and young children, this in itself is very welcome. We then come together and, if we wish, share something of what has arisen for us. Even on the occasions when there is little to share, I find the warm silence of the group
a beautiful space to be in.

Experiment with Light has given me a more focussed and challenging way of listening to 'that of God' within. I have always felt the potential of this Light within to be huge; the challenge remains to realize it more in my life.

John says:

I came to the Experiment with Light as I was leaving the Society of Friends. I had ceased to believe in God, and also in the reality of corporate worship. If I got nothing out of Meeting for Worship, this was in no small measure because I was putting nothing into it.

Whilst Meeting seemed a dead end, the Experiment offered unlimited opportunities. For the first time in years, I was able to experience a universal creative force without feeling I had to cloak that experience in "God language". It was also refreshing to be part of an active seeking community—perhaps we all felt the excitement of the new, containing as it did such a strong connection to George Fox and his message to early Friends.

I find it a challenge to ask a question and then try to wait for an answer without trying to create that answer myself. I struggle to put aside my ego, my thoughts, and my sense of how things are or ought to be. When an answer comes from the Light, however, I know it instantly from one I have created myself. The Light's answer doesn't make sense—at least, not at first. It is sometimes not easily connected to the question I've been asking. It is often an image, either static or moving. And the answer bears repeated exploration: by letting the image continue to "play" like a movie; or by asking "why is it like that?".

The most important insights are those which live with me for days or even weeks afterwards.

When I asked recently about a work issue, the answer leapt out at me: "Because you're invisible". For the rest of the process, I was left asking: how invisible? Because I made myself invisible? Because others did? Because that's how I appear?

Every day, for the next two or three weeks, that phrase "because you're invisible" came to mind. Each time, I would ask for more information. The question of whether the invisibility was caused by me or others was never answered. Eventually the need to know ceased to be important. For instead, over time, ideas for action emerged, both during "thinking time" as well as when I brought the phrase back to subsequent Experiments. Invisible I might be, but that was not how I wished to be. From standing in the Light, I took steps to be visible.

Whenever possible, however, I try not to bring a specific question. Whilst I may not 'get' anything by not bringing an issue into the light, there is a great sense of reassurance and rightness in looking at the Light within. I sense it as a strong pink radiance, centred in my lower torso. At other times, it is like a column going up from my lower torso and out at the top of my head. I feel reassurance, strength, groundedness, and a felt sense of connection to the wider universe.

The radiance also means healing. I have "applied" it to my inflammatory bowel disease, and found relief. I have urged its radiance out from me into the world. And in a way impossible to describe, I have tried to nurture its presence in others dear to me, or those for whom I thought it might be valuable.

At times during the process, I have experienced crushing claustrophobia, in a suffocating or constricting way. Although not physically moving, I would feel as though I was curling up, or that I was growing bigger than my skin would allow. At first I ran from this feeling. I would forcibly break the process of the words, and surface myself by opening my eyes and thinking of other things. Once or twice, I even left the room before the process had finished.

It was Bronwen's suggestion to bring this feeling into the light. That took courage! When the feeling next emerged, I welcomed it as something happening to me for a reason. I brought the light to bear on it, and opened myself to insights about what it might mean for me. I was reconnected to feeling ill and hot as a child. Little by little, the claustrophobia lessened, as did my fear of it. It still recurs occasionally, but through the Experiment I now have a choice about how I respond to it.

We say:

As our group's confidence in the process grew, we no longer felt the need for the taped instructions. We re-wrote and simplified the text. We then switched to using a Tibetan gong sounding at regular intervals, which we later recorded on to a CD. The CD helps us move through the process, but also leaves us free to go at our own pace.

Our group has been a closed group, losing one member (who moved away from the area) and gaining another some time later. Like any group, we have gone through various stages and challenges, but the years of meeting together have brought a particular closeness between us. It feels a very safe space in which to Experiment, and we have been comfortable sharing the strangest, and sometimes most uncomfortable, experiences. We have learnt to hold each other in silence, offering only a rare comment or personal response. Yet the silence is full of Light—and love—and for that we thank our fellow Experimenters.

We made a conscious decision not to be constantly open to new members. However, we have offered a number of introductory sessions to other Friends in our Meeting and encouraged them to set up their own groups. This has been partially successful, although some of these groups have been more short-lived than ours has so far turned out to be. We also learnt that other groups do not always form themselves as easily as ours did.

Although the Experiment is largely a personal journey, an experience which is different from that of the corporate worship of a Quaker meeting, the group setting has become extremely important for us. Quite apart from the regularity it provides, we have felt the presence of others sitting with us; somehow the journey isn't entirely individual. At times we have all felt the need to uphold particular Friends in the group during our regular practice. And when we have facilitated sessions for other Friends, Bronwen has focussed on holding the whole group in the Light.

As the Experiment opened up our spiritual exploring, so too did it open up our understanding of George Fox. As Rex Ambler has written, Fox was not telling the Seekers to believe something, or to say something. He was telling them to *do* something—namely, to wait in the Light.

We have experienced enough of this process to realise that what we have seen is just a glimpse of the Light's potential. If we committed even more to the Experiment and allowed the Light to work within us still further, how much more transformed our lives could become.

Practical Issues

Diana Lampen

Stilling Oneself

Experiment with Light, as articulated by Rex Ambler, is a step-by-step process. The first step, which many Friends find the most difficult, is put thus by George Fox in his letter to Lady Claypole[1]: "Be still and cool in thy own mind and spirit from thy own thoughts…" One Friend told me that he had been coming to Meeting for Worship for about seven years and had still not mastered the skill of letting go of "the chatter in his head".

Tom Fox, the American Friend who was held hostage in Iraq and killed in March 2006, came to an introductory session to the Experiment at Guilford College in 2000. After the practice he was bitterly disappointed that "nothing had happened" as he could not centre down. Then he realised that something had indeed happened; he had been clearly shown that he needed to pay much more attention to this first step of reaching stillness. He went away, and practised and practised. Three years later he attended a five-day retreat at Pendle Hill, the Quaker Study Centre in Pennsylvania, led by Rex with my assistance.[2] Now it was Tom's quiet, deeply centred presence which helped all of us to reach a place of receptive inner stillness. Later still his fellow-hostages who survived paid tribute to Tom as "the most spiritual of us all". He asked them to allow him a time of meditation every day of their captivity, and invited them to join him in the silence.

Many of us have found a valuable "way in" in the teachings of Thich Nhat Hanh, the Buddhist peace campaigner and contemplative, on mindfulness[3]. Mindfulness means being totally present in each moment, whatever one is doing: walking, working, washing the dishes, eating or just sitting. In today's world with all its distractions and pressures we all need, like Tom, to pay attention to the art of becoming still.

Based on that teaching, I offer here a practice which may help you. (Others will discover their own way in.)

[1] *The Journal of George Fox* (ed. John Nickalls, Religious Society of Friends, 1975) page 346

[2] [Our contributors Helene Pollock and Marcelle Martin also attended this seminal event. *Editor.*]

[3] Thich Nhat Hanh: *The Miracle of Mindfulness* (Beacon Press, 1987)

Be sure you are sitting comfortably; it is good to have a straight back—"straight", not rigid. Plant your feet flat on the floor. Rest your hands loosely in your lap. Then go through the body, starting with the feet, and tighten then release each part in turn. Check that you are not frowning or tensing your jaw. When you have gone through the whole body, mentally visit each part again and check that it is still relaxed. Pay special attention to your "tension trouble spots" such as the shoulders.

Then bring your awareness to just outside your nostrils and simply feel the breath. Don't interfere at all, just observe each breath come and each breath go, noting the stronger sensation of the cooler in-breath in the nostrils, the more subtle sensation of the warmer out-breath, and the pauses. The mind will wander a lot at first. Don't be annoyed—that sets up tension! Just let the thought go, focus on the breath again and continue watching.

When you have mastered this watching with total attention, try to be also aware of the slight movements in the body caused by the breath, holding in your awareness at the same time the ebb and flow of air in the nostrils and the gentle body movements. Can you now become aware too of the stillness in the body?

This is deceptively simple but may need a lot of practice, as Tom Fox found. Another Friend who was introduced to it said that he'd been a Quaker for over fifty years, and this was the first time anyone had helped him to centre down.

Thich Nhat Hanh advises us to take frequent pauses in the day to become fully present in this way for just three breaths.[4] You can do this any time, any place: maybe while waiting at red traffic lights, or in the supermarket queue. In an American Quaker school, a few Quaker teachers asked for a minute of mindful silence at the start of each of their classes. The students found this so helpful that the school council petitioned for it to become the custom in every class. Just as pianists and athletes will do some exercises every day even when they have no approaching event, so these brief practices help to keep us attuned to our way of worship.

Once you are able to focus with full attention on the breath, you can add unspoken words which you "say" in time to each breath: one word or syllable on the inhalation, another on the exhalation. I often recommend the phrase "Be still" which is, after all, the first step of Experiment with Light.

[4] *The Miracle of Mindfulness* p.79-80

In your mind you say "Be" as you inhale, and "Still" as you breathe out. Do this again and again until you realise you can let go of the words and open yourself to the Light.

The words of the practice

The Light can be accessed in all sorts of ways—while walking, gardening, painting, even doing the dishes. Experiment with Light is one particular way. What is unique about it? It stems from an attempt to understand how the first Friends worshipped and experienced the Spirit. As he explains in his book *Light to Live By*[5] Rex Ambler was asked the question, "What did they *do* when they waited in the Light?" and discovered that we could see a definite process, which he summed up with the acronym MOWS:

> **M**ind the Light
> **O**pen yourself to what is revealed
> **W**ait
> **S**ubmit to what is being shown (that is, accept, don't resist it)

It is essentially a process of waiting and opening oneself, without taking control or letting one's own thoughts dominate. For this reason it is not just a moment of reconnection with the Light; it needs to be given a period of time free from distractions. Isaac Penington wrote about it: "Wait to feel the light of life [uncovering what is amiss] and drawing [thee] from the evil; and let it choose what it shall please first to discover and draw [thee] from. And though it be little and very inconsiderable in thine eyes, yet dispute not—but where the light first begins to lead, do thou there begin to follow."[6] We have to get our selves out of the way, while always focusing on the Light and what it reveals, which may sometimes be rough and painful. George Fox warns against getting overwhelmed by what we are shown, which can happen if we concentrate too hard on it. He suggests that we turn instead to the illuminating Light: "For looking down at sin and corruption, and distraction, you are swallowed up in it; but looking at the Light that discovers them, you will see over them... and there is the first step to peace."[7]

During Rex's research into early Quaker writing, he was struck by the number of times they described the same experience—that of seeing

[5] Rex Ambler: *Light to Live By* (Quaker books, 2002) pp.1-12

[6] *To all such as complain that they want power* (1662) in Isaac Penington: *The Works* (Quaker Heritage Press 1994-7) vol.ii, p.297

[7] Rex Ambler (ed): *Truth of the Heart: an anthology of George Fox* (Quaker Books, 2001), 1:91

"darkness" in themselves, and then seeing it overcome by the Light. In every case this did not happen immediately, but after a time of waiting. He was then introduced to the work of the Chicago psychologist Eugene Gendlin, which teaches a method called Focusing[8], based on therapeutic experience with psychological problems. Rex was struck by how close it was to what the early Friends described. This helped him to articulate what was happening and offer a clear process to others in the form of what he calls a "guided meditation". (Personally I use the term "practice", as "guided meditation" has been applied to other techniques like visualisations).

It is not surprising that the original words of the practice, as Rex sets them out in *Light to Live By*,[9] are influenced by the Focusing process. Some Friends even call this "the Gendlin version". The method, described by Nancy Saunders in the following chapter, has much to recommend it: the standing back and being somewhat detached (Fox's "Be cool"); letting the issue choose itself; resisting the temptation of answering one's own questions and allowing the answer to come "of itself"; the accompanying bodily sensation which can be so revealing; above all, the fact that it is a *process* through which you move in expectation of a resolution.

But when Light Groups formed to practise the Experiment, they raised two questions about the prompts which Rex suggested. One concerned their apparent emphasis on personal problems and their resolution. The other was about the quantity of words in each of them. Friends often found this original version an excellent introduction because it gives such detailed guidance; but as they became familiar with the practice of waiting in the Light, they did not need such full instructions, which did not always harmonise with the experience they were having. Some preferred a form of wording less psychological in tone and closer to the language of George Fox, so Elizabeth Brown and I developed a new set of prompts. A few people produced their own versions, a popular one being that by Klaus Huber.[10] Others came to a point where they needed no words, just as Isaac Penington wrote, "The end of words is to bring men to the knowledge of things beyond what words can utter."[11] After my Light Group had been meeting for some years, I recorded a version for us in which I simply

8 Eugene Gendlin: *Focusing* (Bantam Books, 1981)

9 *Light to Live By* Appendix 1, p.46. A recent revision is given in the Appendix of this book.

10 See page 100.

11 Undated letter in Isaac Penington: *The Works* (Quaker Heritage Press 1994-7) vol.iii p.457

sounded my Tibetan bell at regular intervals to remind us that this is a process and we should not let ourselves get stuck at any point in it.[12]

As to the first question, we are told in the third of the original prompts to focus on "one thing that gives you a sense of unease". Some Friends have seen this as an expectation that we will always encounter a personal problem, just as early Friends did in many of the accounts which Rex studied. "A grand inquest came upon our whole life: every word, thought and deed was brought to judgement, the root examined and its tendency considered."[13] The prompt reflects this finding and also Gendlin's therapeutic interests. And indeed the Light often shows us some truth about a burden we are carrying, or about something which we are avoiding or not consciously aware of. (Fox calls it "deceit" when we are, as we might say, "kidding ourselves".) When the Light reveals this and brings us to greater clarity, it can be very healing. In Light Groups I have often had to face uncomfortable truths, but I have never felt judged—simply shown something. Over the years this has brought a deepening acceptance of the realities of my own life and reduced my tendency to judge others. Time and again I have ended the practice just recognising that this is how things are.

But we should understand that experiencing what Francis Howgill calls "a long and dark night in which I passed without a guide, and so fell into the pit"[14] does not necessarily imply engaging with our own hang-ups. We may be shown "darkness" in the soul of another person or a social group. We may encounter despair, a loss of trust in the work of the Spirit in the world, a feeling that life is meaningless. This is probably what George Fox famously described as a vision of "an ocean of darkness and death".[15] These different aspects of the darkness are discussed in John Lampen's chapter later in this book.

But early Friends also had other kinds of experience as they waited in the Light, and so do Friends today. Such experiences come as unexpected gifts, and we will want to make sure that the prompts we use do not get in their way. For example, there was one time when I was somewhat unwell and very tired. In the practice I felt that I was being held like a child in its mother's arms, resting and being loved. My husband John once thought at

[12] This version is recorded on CD 4 (see list of resources on page 102).

[13] William Penn: *No Cross, No Crown* (1682) ch.9, §5

[14] *The Inheritance of Jacob* in Hugh Barbour and Arthur Roberts: *Early Quaker Writings* (Eerdmans, 1973) p.175

[15] *The Journal of George Fox* (ed. John Nickalls, Religious Society of Friends, 1975) p.19

the second prompt that he had no current concerns which were claiming attention. He slowly realised that this was because he was being told to prepare for a less active phase in his working life. I have already mentioned what Tom Fox discovered after he had decided that "nothing happened". As I have often said, "If you practice waiting in the Light, expect the unexpected!"

Sometimes the Experiment is a profound and extraordinary experience, sometimes it seems as though very little has been given. We have to learn to accept whatever happens and trust the Light. It may be that we are too tired to be receptive. Perhaps the process simply begins in one session, and we have to pick it up at that point next time. Or we may be approaching it with too much resistance and too little faith. Rex wrote of his own early practice, "...More was needed on my part than the use of a mere skill. There had to be the desire for wholeness and healing, a readiness to face truth that might be painful, and a willingness to let go my ego which so likes to think it has the answers already. I had to accept my own need, and a source of light and life beyond the known limits of my everyday self."[16] Isaac Penington knew the same truth: "Let the light in which thou art begotten to God... be the only judge in thee, and then thou canst not err in judgment. Be not hasty, be not forward in judgment; keep back to the life, still waiting for the appearance and openings of the [new] life. A few steps fetched in the life and power of God are much safer and sweeter than a hasty progress in the hasty, forward spirit."[17]

The gift of the Light may have nothing to do with any current problems. A well-known instance is when George Fox had a series of painful insights into wickedness which felt quite alien to him. He asked God, "Why should I be thus, seeing I was never addicted to commit those evils?" The answer that came was "It was needful that I should have a sense of all conditions, how else should I speak to all conditions?"[18] He was being prepared for a mission quite outside his previous experience. In this way the process may reveal an unforeseen task. Several Friends have told me how they were led unexpectedly into a complete career change. Shelagh Robinson writes later in this book about how Experiment with Light relates to the Quaker understanding of discernment today. To prevent us being wholly focused on ourselves, Rex Ambler also devised sets of prompts which concentrate on the other people in our lives, the groups we belong to

[16] *Light to Live By* p.29

[17] *Some Directions to the Panting Soul* in Isaac Penington: *The Works,* vol.iii, p.207

[18] *Journal* p. 19

(such as our own Quaker meetings), and the situation in the world at large.[19] The sixth stage in each of them is the same: *Consider how you need to act.*

After thinking about these variations, some Friends have tried to formulate a set of prompts to meet their own particular needs. After all, the words are no more than aids, like recipes or prayer books, which are needed less and less as our experience grows. I feel that, if we do this, we need to keep a clear picture of the nature of the process. A dear friend in my Light Group wrote a version of his own, and asked me what I thought of it. It was a beautiful series of quotations to stimulate meditation on nature, our relationships and so on. But it lacked the sense of progression, the **M**inding, **O**pening, **W**aiting and **S**ubmitting, which is the core of this particular method which has to start from our present state of mind and lead after waiting for a time into the gift of a new understanding, resolution and peace. Essential to the Experiment is the surrender of control, exposing ourselves to a deep sense of inner wisdom, and allowing something to happen beyond what we could do for ourselves.

The silence and sharing time

The guidance given by George Fox, Isaac Penington and others is for the individual, whether worshipping in a group or not. Experiment with Light can be practised on one's own, but in many places small "Light Groups" have formed. Just as Meeting for Worship has a different quality from worship on one's own, so does the Experiment. This difference is hard to put into words, but the experiences recounted by many people in this book confirm that it is true.

Friends have often told me of being given a visual or auditory image, and there are several examples in this book. Such experiences go back to the origins of our Society. George Fox "heard" many of his "openings", and also had visions such as seeing an ocean of darkness overcome by an ocean of light and love. It is as if Friends are so accustomed to approaching everything rationally that the Truth has to find an unfamiliar way to make its impact on us. A symbol can communicate in a more complex way than a logical statement; Carl Jung says that "it proceeds of out the confrontation and clash of opposites" and is "an unfathomable mixture of conscious and

[19] These are given in *Light to Live By* Appendix pp.48-53

unconscious factors".[20] This suggests that it can be a reconciliation of things which had been at war in us—at last we are shown a way forward.

This does not often happen to me in this way; but I remember once "hearing" in a Light Group: "Your meeting is living in untruth". I could not understand this at first. Then I received an image, derived from the film *Life is Beautiful.* I was dodging about in a shadowy place, trying to avoid a searchlight beam which was attempting to find me. I suddenly decided that the only thing to do was to stand still and allow the light to catch me. I explored both of these images during some silent time once the guided practice had ended; but it was not until I came home and heard of something which had been happening in my home meeting at the same time that it became clear what I had been told.

Many Light Groups recommend about twenty minutes of silence on one's own after the practice to allow the process to go on working inside us. Sometimes it is only at this point that the meaning of what was shown became clear, as happened to Tom Fox in his first encounter with the practice. Some people use the time to walk in silence, others continue to sit quietly and reflect on what has happened, while some draw a picture or write in a journal. Later in this book Cynthia Jones contributes a poem-meditation written during this time alone.[21]

This is usually followed by a time to share as much or little as each person wants. Naturally this is confidential. It has been found helpful to do this in "worship-sharing" mode, where each person who wants to speak does so when they are ready, and in no particular order. I have sometimes found that by putting my experience into words to share with the others, I have come to understand what it was telling me. The others do not comment on what they hear or discuss it; occasionally someone asks a question so as to understand better. Each contribution is followed by silence. If someone does not want to speak on this occasion, they can still make a valuable contribution to the group by deep prayerful listening.

Sometimes I have found myself not fully "clear" (as George Fox puts it) after my silent time has finished; but as I listen to the others, it throws light on my own experience and clarifies it. This recalls T.S.Eliot's lines[22]:

[20] Carl Jung: *Memories, Dreams Reflections* (Fontana, 1967) p.367

[21] see page 62

[22] *The Dry Salvages II* in T.S.Eliot: *The Complete Poems and Plays* (Faber, 1969) p.186

> *...The sudden illumination—*
> *We had the experience but missed the meaning,*
> *And approach to the meaning restores the experience*
> *In a different form...*

We may each have had very different experiences and yet come to recognise that there has been a common theme, such as "Let something go." This theme does not develop as in a Meeting for Worship where one ministry often sparks off another; it happens at an unspoken level while we are all still in the silence. And after the sharing, the experience may go on working inside for several days.

The sharing time continues the discipline of waiting, not interrupting or trying to interpret another's experience, let alone trying to "fix" their problems. In Experiment with Light, each person must take responsibility for themselves. Though it can be profoundly healing, it is definitely not group therapy, which is where the participants help each other to analyse their problems. Indeed Eugene Gendlin says, "If I were your personal therapist, I would resist the powerful temptation to tell you things, as though I knew more about your problems than you do. But I would not just let you talk either. I would teach you to focus effectively, and I would keep you company as you did so."[23] But occasionally a Light Group has been dominated by one of its members who has deep problems and is trying to use the group to give them the help they need. If this is allowed to happen, it becomes a different kind of group, a support or therapeutic group, but no longer a Light Group; and this can prevent the other members from experiencing the work of the Light in themselves. In Experiment with Light, we give up taking control and allow the Light to do the work.

The procedure is the same in essence but may be different in detail when the group specifically focuses on a problem which they share, or meets to support one of its members who brings a dilemma to the group. Shelagh Robinson discusses this kind of meeting later in this book.

The life of the Light Group

The first Light Groups were formed in Norfolk about ten years ago by Friends who were introduced to the Experiment together and then set up a number of small groups within the same Monthly Meeting. They all met together from time to time to talk about their experiences. They also reported back to the Monthly Meeting occasionally, thus holding

[23] *Focusing* p.11

themselves accountable to the larger body. When people wanted to start a new group in the course of time, one or two Friends from an existing group would offer to join them.

There is no one right way of being a Light Group. Some meet regularly, others less often. Some are closed to visitors and new members, others have an open door. Each Group has to decide how often to meet, who may join, and above all what relationship it should have to the Quaker Meeting which "contains" it. *Quaker Faith and Practice* §12.20 speaks of Meetings growing closer together as worshipping communities and says, "Meeting together in small groups may have its part to play in this process, and may be valuable in helping us to explore and share our spiritual experience." The following section (§12.21) gives some guidelines on how to set up and run such groups. The book makes it fairly clear that these smaller groupings should be careful to enrich the Meeting, not exclude it.

When I joined the Society of Friends, the members of our meeting came from three different towns. During a time of "dryness" in our Meetings for Worship, our elders decided to hold smaller midweek Meetings in each town. As Friends worshipped more often, the quality of the Sunday worship was felt to improve. In the same way, when a number of Friends from one meeting come together as a Light Group, their growing trust in what the Light reveals can be a huge asset to the meeting as a whole, particularly in its Meetings for Business.

But the presence of a Light Group seems to have been divisive in some Meetings,[24] and I feel that Groups should take conscious steps to prevent any feeling of "them and us" from growing. Other Friends in the Meeting may not wish to join and yet feel they are outsiders; so it will be helpful if the Group reports regularly to its Meeting. There is a lot we can learn from those first Light Groups, particularly the openness, accountability, and willingness to leave one's first Group to help another to start. Although it can be a special experience to meet again and again with the same people so that trust and acceptance deepen between them, there are dangers: mutual dependency, too much focus on one member's needs, possible dominance by one or two seasoned Friends with longer experience than the others, repetition and staleness, or the development of patterns which begin to dull the Light. I believe that a Light Group within a Meeting has a responsibility to examine its relationship with its Meeting from time to time. Rex Ambler's "meditation on the Meeting" is helpful in doing this.[25]

The Group I was in for seven years met once a month. It was unusual in having Friends from different Local Meetings. We were never exclusive.

[24] Shelagh Robinson's chapter (pages 42-49) also considers this problem.
[25] *Light to Live By,* p.50

The core members stayed the same, but we had Friends we knew joining us occasionally, and even complete strangers, as we were in easy reach of Woodbrooke, the Quaker Study Centre in Birmingham, and were glad to welcome guests who enquired about the Experiment. The visitors refreshed and enriched the Group. Occasionally their presence may have inhibited someone from speaking about some major personal issue, but it would have been possible for that person to ask the Group for a special meeting if that was so. Our practice was to let the Light guide our meditation, and to trust it and the group present on that day to be open to the work of the Spirit.

It sometimes happens that after a time some people no longer feel the need for a Group. Perhaps issues no longer present themselves "to order" just because the Group is meeting; or the process has become so much a part of their spiritual life that they no longer need regular times of group silence and support. It may be difficult for the others when a member decides to leave the Group. Even an inevitable change of job or address will disturb the balance that has grown up, and might lead to the end of the Group. But we should remember that the Light Group, and indeed the practice itself, are only tools and not ends in themselves. Experience suggests that Light Groups, like other groups, have a life-cycle of birth, growth, maturity, and then a gradual fading of energy and commitment. It may be right to lay it down; the struggle to keep it going may be a wrong use of one's resources. It seems to me that what happens at this stage is that its members carry with them a heightened sense of trust in waiting and the guidance of the Spirit into their meetings and other aspects of their lives, like seeds carried on the wind.

But though we can learn to dispense with Light Groups, for many of us it has been an indispensable stage on the way. As Robert Barclay found:[26]

> God not only reveals himself in each individual, but is in the midst of the group as well. Each one partakes not only of the particular strength and refreshment which comes from the good in himself, but shares with that of the whole body. Being a living member of the body, he has joint fellowship and communion with all. If this form of worship is continued faithfully, it becomes easy, though it is very difficult at first.

[26] Dean Freiday: *Barclay's Apology in Modern English* (Dean Freiday, 1967) p.255 (Prop.XI, §8)

Focusing on the Light

Nancy Saunders[1]

> What is here urged are inward practices of the mind at deepest levels, letting it swing like the needle, to the polestar of the soul.
>
> Thomas R.Kelly, *A Testament of Devotion*

One of the most important responsibilities of a member of the Religious Society of Friends is to lead one's life in ways that enhance the ability to experience the Light within.

In my own development as a Quaker, there have been three particularly helpful influences on this aspect of my spiritual growth. One of these was a relatively brief, but very powerful relationship with a Quaker spiritual nurturer who helped me remember to turn and return to the Light within. Another is the Simplicity Testimony that encourages me to eliminate as much clutter from my life as possible, so that I can hear the still, small voice.

The third influence, which is the topic of this chapter, is a practice which I have been doing for many years which provides a step-by-step process for finding the place of inner truth that precedes language and other forms of symbolic expression. This process was developed by a University of Chicago philosophy professor and psychologist, Eugene Gendlin, and grew, in part, out of his experience of sitting in Meeting for Worship at Pendle Hill when he was a young man. He gave the name "Focusing" to this process. In conversation with me he said, "Focusing arises from within a deep tradition that Quakers preserve for the world."

Focusing consists of a set of specific steps for finding an inner place, a silent place of deep bodily knowing that precedes thought and symbolic expression, and constitutes a person's most basic experience of their situation.

A fruitful way of thinking about the relationship between the silent worship of Quakerism and Focusing is to imagine two overlapping circles: there is an area of commonality and two areas of complementarity.

[1] An earlier form of this chapter appeared in *Friends Journal*, January 2003. It was a challenge to write, and I am grateful to the following people for their helpful comments: Clarence Oakley, Eugene Gendlin, Arlene Kelly, Marcelle Martin, Mac Given, John Wenderoth and Hillel Felder.

The commonality between Focusing and Quakerism includes six elements

- Truth resides within each person, rather than in external authority;
- Truth can be experienced directly by a person without the need for an intermediary, either human or symbolic;
- Truth is larger, deeper and more fundamental than any symbolic expression;
- every single person is valuable;
- the capacity for on-going growth and development is inherent within human beings;
- human beings are designed to be present with one another.

In addition, the centrality of bodily experience in Focusing is an element that early Friends took for granted in their religious lives, but is probably less available to present day Friends[2].

The way that Focusing complements my religious life as a Friend is that it provides a specific, Quaker-friendly practice that I can use in addressing the problems of every day life, so that more of my energy is available for living my ministry, rather than being diverted to preoccupation with personal problems. As I introduce the reader to the six steps of the Focusing process, I will give an example of each step from my own experience to assist the reader in their understanding. My experience is printed in italics.

Clear a Space In this step the Focuser acknowledges one by one the problematic concerns of daily life, without engaging emotionally with them. As each concern comes into awareness, the Focuser greets it in an accepting way, and puts it aside temporarily. *a) I'm worried about my daughter who hasn't called for several weeks; why doesn't she call me? b) I'm trying to lose five pounds and limiting my food intake feels very unpleasant. c) I made a commitment to a friend and now I want to change my mind; I feel bad about this.*

Felt Sense From the assortment of concerns, the Focuser chooses one, and without thinking about or analyzing the problem, scans within his or her body in order to experience the body's wordless expression of that concern. Some people find this step very easy, while others need more support and assistance in learning to find the felt sense. *I decide to Focus on the concern about weight loss. Without analyzing the problem I turn my attention to the subtle, somewhat vague sensations in my body, and notice a feeling of discomfort in the region of my midriff.*

[2] see Scott Martin, "Quaking and the Rediscovery of Primitive Quakerism" (*Friends Journal*, May 2001)

Get A Handle The Focuser seeks for a word, image or phrase that captures the essence of the felt sense. The handle almost always expresses something sensory, like "tight", "jiggly", "jumpy", "hot", &c. *I try out a few different handles: "broken", "shattered", "in pieces".*

Resonate The Focuser matches the handle with the felt sense, to see if the handle really fits the felt sense. If it does, the Focuser experiences the feeling of that fit; if it doesn't the Focuser tries another handle until one does really fit. *The words "in pieces" fits the felt sense very well. I let myself appreciate that fit.*

Ask In this step the Focuser poses one or more questions to the felt sense and its handle, in order to bring the deepest meaning of the felt sense into conscious awareness. For example, a question might be: "What makes this problem so Jittery (the handle)?" Another might be "What does this jittery feeling need?" *I ask "What is it within me that is in pieces?" I very quickly become aware that while my life is very full I keep the different aspects of my life quite separate from each other. The result is that the richness of my life doesn't nourish me as well as it might.*

Receive In this step the Focuser experiences an internal shift, whereby the beginning concern is eased and a fresh understanding emerges. The Focuser can either stop at this point or repeat the steps with another aspect of concern. *I feel a sense of relief: the discomfort disappears and I have the beginnings of clarity about some changes I need to make in my life.*

Although I originally learned these steps from the small book entitled *Focusing*[3] and practiced it by myself for many years, I have since participated in programs offered by the Focusing Institute in New York City and now much prefer to do Focusing with a partner. In addition I have been a participant in Changes Groups sponsored by the Focusing Institute, which are comparable in many ways to the Experiment with Light Groups.

Focusing with a partner brings with it a respectful intimacy with another person that is certainly missing in most of our social relationships and very often missing in our emotionally intimate relationships with family members and friends. My own experience of Focusing with a partner is that it allows me to glimpse the delicate mystery of another human being and leads me to feel more connected and tolerant in all of my relationships. I

[3] Eugene Gendlin: *Focusing* (Bantam Books, 1981)

feel less distracted by peoples' personalities and more able to experience them on a deeper level. For Friends, who place such a high value on community, Focusing provides a mechanism for moving beyond tolerance to true spiritual intimacy, both in the context of the Meeting and in our relationships with the larger community. A recent example of this is the role I played in my Meeting in responding to a Friend whose behavior had become very disruptive and was consuming a great deal of the Meeting's energy. Through Focusing I realized that the Meeting lacked the formal structure for dealing with the problem and that we needed to create one. The Meeting accepted this, and the situation became much more manageable.

My Focusing experiences usually bring a sense of surprise, since the deep pre-language knowing of the felt sense very often produces a vastly different way of approaching life from the customary busy activity of conscious thinking. Invariably, the understanding and consequent actions that proceed from the felt sense seem clearer and deeper than the understanding and actions that proceed from logical thought. One's experience after a Focusing session is often "I had no idea that was in there, but I know it's true."

Isaac Penington confirms this in religious terms: "When the principle of life is known and that which God hath begotten [is] felt in the heart, the distinction between what God opens and requires there and what springs up in man's wisdom, reason and imagination, is very manifest."[4] George Fox seems to have had similar experiences. He described how "One morning, as I was sitting by the fire, a great cloud came over me, and a temptation beset me; but I sat still... And as I sat still under it and let it alone, a living hope arose in me and a true voice... And immediately the cloud and temptation vanished away, and life arose over it all, and my heart was glad, and I praised the living God."[5]

Another characteristic feature of a Focusing session is that it always produces a subtle physical change, perhaps a slight blush, a sigh, tears, or the release of muscular tension. This change is not deliberately produced by the person, but rather wells up from deep inside. I know first hand that the physical shift has a spiritual quality to it, and it brings to mind a passage

[4] *Some Questions and Answers shewing Mankind his Duty* in Isaac Penington: *The Works* (Quaker Heritage Press 1994-7) vol.ii, p.276

[5] *The Journal of George Fox* (ed. John Nickalls, Religious Society of Friends, 1975) page 25

from Barclay's *Apology*: "The soul has its own sense as well as the body. And that is why David, when he wants us to know what divine goodness is, calls not for speculation, but sensation: 'taste and see that the Lord is good' (*Psalm 34:8*). The best and truest knowledge of God is not that which is wrought by the labour and sweat of the brain, but that which is kindled within us, by a heavenly warmth in our hearts."[6] Focusing seems to bring one closer to a point of spiritual alchemy, whereby body transmutes into soul and soul into body.

I know that some Friends are concerned that paying attention to one's own problems is a form of self-indulgence, and that a person's time and energy are better spent serving the world. My own experience is that Focusing not only releases more of my energy for service, but that it helps me to choose the forms of service that are really right for me. As an example I was recently asked by the Nominating Committee of my Meeting to serve as Assistant Clerk for a year and then take of the role of Clerk. My initial reaction was to think about all of the responsibilities of my life, and conclude that there was no way I could take on these roles. After a day or so of Focusing practice, however, I realized that in fact the roles of Assistant Clerk and then Clerk are exactly right for me at this point in my life.

Focusing has been an invaluable resource to me on my spiritual journey, and I am grateful for the opportunity to introduce it to other Friends. I am also deeply grateful to all of those in Experiment with Light groups who have brought together Quaker spirituality and the principles of Focusing.

[6] Dean Freiday: *Barclay's Apology in Modern English* (Dean Freiday, 1967,) p.25 (Prop.II §8)

Practising Discernment

Shelagh Robinson

Our understanding of our faith often begins with an exploration of Advices and Queries; indeed this small booklet is an unfailing guide throughout all our journey towards and with God. But the introduction to Advices and Queries reminds us in the words of the Elders of Balby written in 1656 that these advices are not laid upon us as "a rule or form to walk by, but that all, with the measure of light that is pure and holy, may be guided and so in the light walking and abiding, these may be fulfilled in the Spirit, for the letter killeth but the Spirit giveth life."[1]

This advice reminds us that even when we are most certain and most wisely advised we have the responsibility to discern, to find our own way to the truth. "Every one is to be in it. And to walk in the truth, and in the spirit, and to come to the truth in their own particulars.... And so none can worship the God of truth but who come to the truth in their own hearts."[2]

A faith community without hierarchy, without creed or catechism but claiming the possibility of direct personal experience of the divine, whether this is interpreted as a deep mystical experience, informed conscience, the recognition of that of God in ourselves and the other, or indeed all of these, requires checks and balances that enable us to test the authenticity of our experience. Members of those faiths with catechisms and creeds are supported in their spiritual development with clear guidelines, with detailed maps for the journey that in principle at least do not allow for deviations from the routes laid down by leaders. Friends experience is different. We are supported on our journeys by the experiences of those who have trod similar paths; some of long experience; others new to the journey; but all with valid contributions to make. Our journeying is that of travellers who meet along the road to exchange travellers' tales that will perhaps smooth a path or point a different way.

The need for discernment is not unique to Friends. The discernment process of the Roman Catholic Society of Jesus (Jesuits) involves members of the community with a decision to make being required to present the arguments of the position they oppose. Again in Roman Catholicism in the process of canonisation a devil's advocate is appointed to argue against the proposed candidate for sainthood. This adversarial process is not in the ways of

[1] *Quaker Faith and Practice* (Britain Yearly Meeting, 1995) 1.01
[2] George Fox in Rex Ambler: *Truth of the Heart* (Quaker Books, 2007). 1.34

Friends: ours is a gentle process of quiet waiting, of using the tried and tested ways of discernment. It is essentially a sifting process, a process of discarding what is not necessary, and by doing so to reach a clarity, a lightness in which the Spirit can fly free. Discernment and discarding are closely linked. The cook making a perfect stock, skims and skims and skims until all that is not needed has been discarded. Our physical bodies in the process of digestion discard what is not needed or might be harmful, and the roots of the words for these processes are the same.

We see discernment in action in all our corporate actions. It is present in the attentive listening of our clerks as they seek the sense of the Meeting, it is there when the minute is laid before the Meeting for amendment or assent. Our nominations process is in itself a process of discernment, of testing the names that arise by consultation and discussion but most importantly in an atmosphere of prayer, following this process faithfully until we find the right Friend to fulfil the allotted task. The same is true in accepting a new member of our Society. The right holding of Meeting for Worship requires the discernment of the individual worshipping Friend. "Is this ministry for me or is it for the Meeting? Is this the right time to minister or is this a time to wait? Is this gathered silence one that should not be broken?" The exercise of eldership during Meeting for Worship should be subject to the discernment process. Does the situation need the gentle check of eldership or is it better left for a different solution? What does love require—love for the individual and love for the whole Meeting? One of the most important queries in the Quaker discernment process is probably "What does love require?"

But our processes and structures, however rightly ordered, are only a container for the transformative experience of the divine encounter. Discernment becomes more intensely personal when we are led by the spirit into living a faithful life. Our response to the call to live by the Quaker testimonies is made more complex by the complexities of modern living. How do we live out our testimony to peace, to simplicity, to equality, to truth and integrity and to the growing awareness of the need for a testimony to the earth?

John Punshon wrote,

> Newcomers to the Society are often attracted by our values and practices, like peace work, simplicity of life and the pursuit of integrity. They are soon told that these are 'testimonies' They then find that there is no authoritative statement of what the testimonies are, only hallowed examples of their applications in particular circumstances. They find that Friends debate the demands which the clearly recognised testimonies make on people, and also what new testimonies there ought to be. Thus they find that the testimonies

> are what Quakers stand for. They are religious, ethical, collective, demanding—and vague.[3]

It is in this area of vagueness that personal discernment is of most value, as we ask how does this testimony apply to me and in what way am I called to be faithful to it? Am I called to make fundamental changes in my life or to acts of small quiet faithfulness? How do I make the words on the page become something I know experientially and live faithfully? The question is not what we believe is happening when we discern, but what the experience is of that process.

Within our faith community we have many practices that enrich our discernment. Paradoxically the Meeting for worship that brings us the first stirrings of a leading to a different faithfulness is also the place where we test that leading as we wait on the movement of the Spirit. This is and has always been the way of Friends: "If the kingdom of heaven was literally coming into being, then their task was to live in the kingdom now, to help to bring it about. Friends searched for the truth by 'waiting in the light'. What they discovered in that waiting was then lived out in their lives; this was their witness or testimony to the truth they had discovered."[4]

Friends have always supported each other's discernment processes, both individually and corporately. As we seek to know each other in the eternal ways we often find ourselves part of one another's discernment. Simple, personal friendship becomes deep spiritual companionship when relationships are opened to the movement of the Spirit and what comes naturally into being may be slightly formalised by making specific opportunities to ask "How is the Spirit working in your life?" We cannot overvalue the richness of these relationships and the extent to which they support our faithful living.

We have tools of discernment like the support groups, sometimes called Faithfulness Groups, where a group of Friends are called together to support the work and witness of an individual Friend on a regular basis or over a time limited period. These groups with their mixture of gentle challenge and questions, and prayerful loving caring enrich both the Friend who is the focus of the group and the members.

In recent years Clearness Groups have come back into more regular use. Originally used by early Friends to test whether couples seeking to marry were ready and clear to do so, they are now used frequently throughout

[3] John Punshon: *Testimony and Tradition* (Quaker Home Service, 1990) p.19
[4] Marion McNaughton in *Engaging with the Quaker Testimonies; a Tool Kit* (Quaker Books 2007) p.7

Britain Yearly Meeting and beyond to help individual Friends and Meetings come to or towards clearness on difficult issues. Set in the context of deep worship a Meeting for Clearness seeks to help the discernment by a process of simple questioning around the topic.

The kinds of dilemma that can be brought to a Meeting for Clearness are wide ranging. Decisions to accept challenging roles in the Society, or to ask for release from such roles; the challenge of leaving full time employment to be free for adventurous living, to marry, to enter a committed relationship, to leave a committed relationship; all these have been the subject of Meetings for Clearness. A Meeting in conflict over a long period of time may seek a Clearness Meeting to discern the right way forward.

A Meeting for Clearness is not a quick fix, the issue may need to be returned to again and again until the right degree of clarity has been arrived at. The core of the Clearness process is that it takes place in the context of worship, it is not primarily a discussion and though the mind is used in the accurate framing of the questions asked, the process is one of openness to the leadings of the spirit. The pivotal questions in a Meeting for Clearness come from the same place that true ministry comes; it comes with that same feeling of awe and tentativeness, with the slight shift in the body that signals that we have entered a different space. Having been part of the process I have been left with the questions "Where did that come from? What led me to that place?" and I recognise that I have been in the place of mystery, far beyond intellect and reason. As we make prayerful discernment part of our lives, the testing becomes natural, not arid scrupulousness but a lightness of heart and spirit as we learn what it is to live according to God's will and thus approach wholeness.

Added to these familiar ways of discernment the practice that Rex Ambler has called Experiment with Light has become a precious and important part of personal discernment for many Friends. Sometimes this practice has been given other names such as "Wait in the Light", but the variations have always seemed to me to lose something of the essence of the process. When George Fox declared "And this I knew experimentally" he used the 17th century understanding of the word which is closer to our use of the word "experience"; but Experiment with Light is both experience and experiment and the process is more fully captured when we use the original name.

How does this practice fit in the overall picture of Quaker discernment processes?

Light Groups are not Meetings for Clearness, although occasionally the clarity that is experienced during a Light Group may have something of the same quality; nor are they Meetings for Worship, although the depth of silence may be akin to a Meeting for Worship. Meditation, even when done as part of a group, is essentially a solitary process. Friends may use meditation techniques to enable them to settle into worship; but to remain in a meditative state throughout worship is to hinder the Gathered Meeting which essentially is a corporate opening out to God. If we remain in our own space in meditation then we lose the corporate experience. Light Groups are not primarily Support Groups/Faithfulness Groups although as the bonds develop between group members mutual support and understanding is a strong side shoot of the experience.

I have always seen Light Groups as one of the richest ways of "coming to Meeting with heart and mind prepared." They provide a significant tool for understanding the barriers that arise out of our personal circumstances, out of our ego, out of our physical state; the things that get in the way of our wholeness.

As a supervisor of counselling therapists I know from deep experience that there are times when I need to let my supervisees work to clear their own issues before they are clear to address their client work. In my client work I know that we will experience times of stuck-ness when the therapy seems to be going round in circles and I have learned to stay with the stuck-ness, to accept it and see where it takes me. All of us have experienced in our own lives, the surprising return of painful past issues that we thought had been fully dealt with. In our Spiritual journey we find ourselves back with doubts, with periods of aridness that we felt we had overcome, back with the familiar struggle to accept those whose very presence seems a barrier to our growth—while perhaps remembering that we in our turn may be that barrier to others—and there is need to accept this.

Finding ourselves needing to wrestle with past issues can be the start of a whole new understanding. Coming back to the beginning with new recognition is one of the discernments of Experiment with Light; is one of the experiences of the spiritual journey across all traditions:

> *We shall not cease from exploration*
> *And the end of all our exploring*
> *Will be to arrive where we started*
> *And know the place for the first time.*[5]

But here is an important balance to be found between accepting that some issues will re-surface and an ego-driven need to stay in the hard places

[5] *Little Gidding V* in T.S.Eliot: *The Complete Poems and Plays* (Faber, 1969) p.197

rather than accept the challenge of moving on. Light Groups are not therapy groups and they are most surely not "stuck" therapy groups. When groups have drifted into being poor imitations of therapy groups they become unsatisfactory and usually fail. If other members of the Meeting suspect that the Light Group is somehow straying into practices that properly belong in therapy, this raises doubts and concerns that isolate the group and its members from the Meeting.

Fears have been expressed about the potential damage the Light Group might cause vulnerable individuals. In fact, for the majority of Friends our common experience is that whenever we open ourselves to the movement and power of the Spirit and in whatever context—on a Woodbrooke course, participating in an exercise at a Conference, during a Meeting for Clearness—we can find ourselves vulnerable. Margaret Fell's reminder that the Light will rip us open remains part of our experience as Friends. But the ripping open, albeit painful and frightening, splits us as the seed splits in the process of new growth. It can and frequently does happen in Light Groups or during the solo practice of the meditation as the personal stories in this book reveal; but we may safely trust the process and remember that within the Society there are many tried and tested resources for support and help during times of spiritual vulnerability. Being part of a Light Group often provides the necessary support, though it is important to remember that the other resources are also there for us.

There are other concerns that have given rise to serious difficulties between Light Groups and Local and Area Meetings; the perception that the Light Group is exclusive and therefore a source of division in the Meeting; the perception that to its members the Light Group is of a higher priority than Meeting for Worship or other Meeting activity; the perception that Friends involved in Experiment with Light see themselves as more spiritual, a higher or more refined Quaker. Factions arise that are potentially damaging to the life of the Meeting and deeply hurtful to all involved. Those who have experienced being part of a Light Group value the insights and growth points that come from the regular shared practice of the meditation but it seems important that a group that in essence is a tool of discernment should reflect with discernment on itself. A group that lets the Light illuminate its own process and role. Anne Hosking has written, "Unless you change in response to what you see, then it is just another meditation, and that would be an untruth... Truth leads us to be whole people, without deluding ourselves, without hypocrisy—as moderns would say, with integrity, or as Fox said, 'being single before the Lord'. We need to tread and trample all deceit under foot in ourselves, then 'things may be spoken in nakedness of heart, one to another'."[6]

A useful check list for a Light Group based on a Pendle Hill Pamphlet[7] is:-

Where is the Spirit in this matter?
Are we coming from a centred place, or are we reacting to our own unresolved issues?
Are our personalities or ego affecting the way this group is perceived from outside?
Is this group a gift to the wider Meeting community?
Are we a prayed for, prayerful, and prepared group open to continual discernment and guidance?

These questions could help to ground the group and recognise its place in a wider context.

I continue to be amazed, and deeply thankful for the way Experiment with Light opens us to new understandings, to new discernments of what gets in the way of our wholeness. On a Woodbrooke course where the meditation was offered the following poem was shared. It seems to me to demonstrate very simply how the process works, how it develops beyond the actual experience of the meditation and how the understanding that is reached can be worked on in the future, should this be necessary.[8]

What I found was fear.
And yes, I know the psycho answers
But it scared me

A serpent, coiled and threatening
To spring on me unsuspecting
And squeeze the light out of my life.

So I held it in the light

But it wouldn't go away
So I took it for a walk
And the sun blessed my face
And geese stood proud at the pond
Where some kids had a sail boat
And I listened to my steps
Sounding strong.

[6] Anne Hosking, articles in *The Friend* 19.2.1999 and 5.3.1999

[7] Margery Mears-Larrabbee *Spirit Led Eldering – Integral to our Faith and Practice* (Pendle Hill Pamphlet 392, 2007)

[8] by Sue Laidly – reproduced with permission.

Later, when I looked again
The serpent didn't seem so scary.
In fact, it had fallen asleep and seemed
Somewhat shrunken.
So I left it there.

George Fox expressed the same experience in the words and tone of the 17th Century: "For the first step to peace is to stand still in the light (which discovers things contrary to it) for power and strength to stand against that nature which the light discovers: for here grace grows, here is God alone glorified and exalted and the unknown truth, unknown to the word made manifest." [9]

In the personal discernment experience of the 21st Century the Light reveals the serpent of fear and as its power diminishes, God is exalted and made manifest in the playing children, the proud stance of the geese, the openness to the blessing of the sun and the recognition of personal strength. The Light that rips us open also brings healing and peace.

[9] *Truth of the Heart* 1.89

Experiencing Darkness in Experiment With Light

John Lampen

Experiment with Light is a practical step-by-step process offering people the experience which early Friends sought and found in their worship, experience of the insight-giving, healing and empowering work of the Holy Spirit in their hearts. Modern psychology has shed new light on our unconscious minds, and the question has been raised whether Experiment with Light is "dangerous". The same thing tends to be asked whenever a new meditation or group encounter process is developed. It probably arises from the natural reluctance we feel in facing issues which we have repressed or avoided. We fear that after the lid is raised we cannot put the contents back in the jar, and once they get out they can do harm. This anxiety must be taken seriously. In the case of the Experiment it has been raised by trained counsellors and therapists during introductory workshops and sessions; and also some people have reported an overwhelming awareness of darkness or evil while doing the practice which was hard to surmount. In this chapter, I shall look at the question first in its early Quaker context, and then briefly discuss the relationship of Experiment with Light to mental disturbance and therapy.

George Fox's experience of the darkness

The first thing to note about this encounter with darkness[1] is that George Fox, speaking from experience, told us it would happen.

> The Lord doth show unto man his thoughts, and discovereth all the secret workings in man. A man may be brought to see his evil thoughts and running mind and vain imaginations, and may strive to keep them down and to keep his mind in, but cannot overcome them. . . [2]

He says that there are three ways in which darkness may be encountered. The first is that it appears as what he calls "addictions".

> Whatever it is you are addicted to that's where the tempter will get you. If he can trouble you there he gets an advantage over you, and then you are finished.[3]

Fox uses this term rather than "sin" or "vices" because it has a wider meaning, including all the ways in which we may fail or fall short of the Truth available to us:

[1] See Paul Buckley "*Darkness* in the Journal of George Fox" (*Quaker Religious Thought* 2001, vol.30 no.2)

[2] *The Journal of George Fox* ed John Nickalls (Religious Society of Friends 1952, p.58)

[3] *Truth of the Heart* 1:90 in Rex Ambler's rendering

> So long as people's minds are involved with material things, with things that have been made and so are liable to change, and so long as they are involved with religions and ways of life that are similarly changeable and with unreliable teachers, their minds are enslaved. And they are insecure and unstable, tossed up and down with windy doctrines and thoughts, ideas and things, because their minds have abandoned the dependable Truth in their own inner being...[4]

We long to be free of our addictions, but lack the strength to leave them behind. Fox tells how, as a young man,

> I found that there were two thirsts in me, the one after [created things] to have gotten health and strength there, and the other after the Lord the Creator and his son Jesus Christ. And I saw all the world could do me no good. If I had had a king's diet, palace and attendance, all would have been as nothing, for nothing gave me comfort but the Lord by his power. And I saw professors, priests and people were whole and at ease in that condition which was my misery, and they loved that which I would have been rid of.[5]

Secondly we may feel a great pressure of external evil, either as a menacing presence or as the weight of all that is wrong in the world, which it seems can never be righted. During a severe illness, John Woolman dreamed of an aged negro being hanged so that his meat might feed a strange animal of mixed breed, watched by the guests at a tea-party. He was powerless to intervene; he could only stand by and weep. The dream seemed to sum up the whole burden of the institution of slavery against which he struggled, as it seemed to him, to so little effect.[6]

And George Fox recalled:

> There the Lord shewed me that the natures of those things which were hurtful [in the world] were within, in the hearts and minds of wicked men... And I cried to the Lord saying, "Why should I be thus, seeing I was never addicted to commit those evils?" And the Lord answered that it was needful I should have a sense of all conditions, how else should I speak to all conditions; and in this I saw the infinite power of God.[7]

The third way in which we encounter the dark is in the feeling that life is meaningless. In this condition, our efforts do not merely seem futile because the task is so large. We no longer believe there is any reason for undertaking them, because all sense of value is lost.

[4] *Truth of the Heart* 1:10

[5] *Journal* p.12

[6] *The Journal and Major Essays of John Woolman* ed. Phillips Moulton, (Friends United Press, 1971) p.161.

[7] *Journal* p.19

> A voice said to me, "All things come [simply] by nature", and I was quite overshadowed by it.[8]

> You see little and know little and have little, and see your emptiness and...your nakedness and barrenness and unfruitfulness and... the hardness of your hearts and your own unworthiness...[9]

Fox thought that this encounter with darkness was inevitable, in at least one of its forms, but he was also convinced by his experiences that it was only the beginning of a process ("There is the first step to peace"[10]). If we do not take fright at this stage, we will inevitably be guided to the next stage, though it may need more than one time of practice before we are fully "clear" or freed from what is negative. Fox maintains that this awareness is a product of the Light (for in darkness we can see nothing clearly) and is the evidence that there is a power which is coming to our help.

> But oh! that's when I saw my troubles and tribulations more than I have ever done before! As the Light appeared, everything that was out of the Light also appeared: darkness, death, temptations, whatever was not right and good. Everything was seen and disclosed in the Light. . . And then I received a spiritual discernment which enabled me to discern my own thoughts, longings and desires, and to see what it was that obscured my vision and what opened it up.[11]

Fox offers a definite technique to use when this happens:

> When the Light discloses and reveals things to you, things that tempt you, confuse you, distract you and the like, don't go on looking at them but look at the Light that has made you aware of them. And with this same Light you will feel yourself rising above them and empowered to resist them.[12]

The urge towards death

For one or two people this dark experience has brought a sense of personal death. One person reported that she was told to kill herself. It is important not to belittle such experiences and not to offer a bland interpretation. The urge is real; but if Experiment with Light starts by showing us the dark places in our minds before it guides us forward, there is no reason to conclude that such commands come from the deepest Truth within us. And here too we find that Fox has been in the same place before us. As a young

[8] *Journal* p 25.

[9] George Fox: *Epistle 16* (1652)

[10] *Truth of the Heart* 1:91

[11] *Truth of the Heart* 1:75

[12] *Truth of the Heart* 1:91

man he was tempted to suicide, as the following passage from a letter, written much later, shows.

> Ye that have been in the wilderness can witness this *with me*, and the same temptations, even to despair and *to make themselves away.* [13]

Note that he calls the urge to suicide a "temptation". That is, it comes from the devil "a murderer from the beginning, the corrupter of humankind".[14] Fox is alone among commentators, I think, in identifying his suicidal thoughts with Jesus' temptation on the pinnacle of the temple in *Matthew* 4:5. This seems bizarre at first, but there is a psychological insight in it; it is as if Satan is saying to Jesus: "Now jump! If God saves you, that will prove he has a mission for you. If he doesn't, it's better for you to die now."

But sensing a need to die may not be a temptation of this kind. It can also have another meaning . The Light may be pointing us to a stage in the spiritual journey. Fox writes:

> But all you that be in your own wisdom and in your own reason, you tell that silent waiting on God is famine to you. It is a strange life to you to come to be silent; you must come into a new world. Now you must die in the silence, die from [your] wisdom, die from [your] knowledge, die from [your] reason and die from [your] understanding.[15]

The repeated heavy emphasis on the word "die" should make that clear that Fox is not just warning us to become less self-centred or self-confident. Death surely symbolises more than a change in our way of thinking. It points to a giving-up of everything, a state of non-being, which is necessary before there can be a new birth; as Paul says mysteriously in *Colossians* 3:3, "For ye are dead, and your life is hid with Christ in God." This "death" is the time of stillness or waiting to which Fox repeatedly refers, a time in which "you see little, and know little, and have little, and see your emptiness and see your nakedness". He warns us that "the husbandman waits patiently after the seed is sown; there is a winter before the summer comes." Stephen Crisp, another early Friend, tells how he could not still his mind in worship and come to the light.

> At length, I thought to go forth; and as I was going, the Lord thundered through me, saying That which is weary must die. So I turned to my seat and waited in the belief of God for the death of that part which was weary of the work of God.[16]

[13] *Epistle 45*, (1653); my italics. I am grateful to Lewis Benson for drawing my attention to this passage.

[14] *Truth of the Heart* 1:48

[15] *Truth of the Heart* 1:63, original text

[16] *The Journal of the life of Stephen Crisp* (1694), p.18

If thoughts of death come up during the practice, we do not have to strain to discover if this is what they signify. If we trust the process, if we wait in the Light, it will make it clear what they mean for us. In his illness John Woolman had another dream, in which he was in a mass of "human beings in as great misery as they could be and live, and… I was mixed in with them so that henceforth I might not consider myself as a distinct or separate being." Then he heard an angelic voice saying, "John Woolman is dead". In the morning he even asked his wife if she knew who he was, and was told "John Woolman". As he pondered on his dream, words of Paul's were given to him, "I am crucified with Christ, nevertheless I live; yet not I, but Christ liveth in me" (*Galatians* 2:20) and this showed him that the angel's words proclaimed the death of his own will.[17]

Therapy and Experiment with Light

> Therefore be still a while from your own thoughts, your own searching, seeking, desiring, imagining, and rest on the divine source within you, so as to rest your mind on God himself. You will then find strength from him and find him to be a present help in time of trouble.[18]

In this and many other passages, George Fox makes clear that he is recommending a process. As we have seen when considering thoughts of death, there is one possible wrong turning which may be taken in it— when we attempt to think through the problem of our inner darkness for ourselves, instead of waiting for the Light to reveal what is wrong in our lives and to show the way out of it. "You must be kept from asserting your own will, that is, the merely human part of you, then you will feel the power of God that will set [human] nature on its [true] course."[19] If this trap is avoided, the process leads us on to its goal:

> If you go on loving and obeying [the Light] it will lead you out of darkness and out of your wrongdoing, into the light of life, into the way of peace, and into the life and power of Truth.[20]

Difficulties can be expected if we embark on the journey without real trust in the process. Like many worthwhile things the journey through the sense of darkness may be unpleasant or worse. Margaret Fell spoke of being "ripped open by the Light". Courage to continue comes from faith in the power of the Light to guide and heal us. I do not wish to limit the power of

[17] Woolman: *Journal* p.186
[18] *Truth of the Heart* 1:61
[19] *Truth of the Heart* 1:127
[20] *Truth of the Heart* 1:128

the Spirit, but I hesitate to recommend the Experiment to someone with personal burdens who seemed to be clutching at any straw to find relief.

I once heard a Cherokee elder speak at Appalachian Yearly Meeting. Someone asked him about traditional healing, and he said, "If I break my leg and need to get it fixed, of course I phone for an ambulance. But if I really need *healing* I go to my own people." I think it is sensible to apply this wisdom to Experiment with Light. I know occasions when the practice has had a deeply healing effect. But if you have a clinical depression or a personality disorder, don't look on the Experiment as a substitute for consulting the doctor, and getting the appropriate medical help. The untreated problem might interfere with your practice in the Light; and you may well put an unfair burden on the small support group, who are there to share, listen and encourage but not to provide amateur group therapy. In Experiment with Light each person is responsible for herself or himself.

I have shared these thoughts with a group who had just begun to practice the Experiment, which included a psychiatrist and several therapists and counsellors. All affirmed that they found it a very safe process, because there was no human therapist to force disclosure and impose interpretations to meet the demands of a particular theory or system. There was no pushing of people into a level of awareness which they could not tolerate. The ego's mechanisms of defence were not being overridden. The small group could affirm and support, but nobody had to disclose more than they found comfortable. And when one practice left someone with "unfinished business", it was possible for them to take it back into the next practice and gain insights at their own pace.

Experimenting is one example of "living adventurously", and no adventure can be risk-free. But if lasting difficulties arise, they are likely to come from a failure to trust the Spirit enough to go through the darkness into a new light. As with mediation, psychotherapy and other experiential processes, the failure to see a problem through can aggravate it instead of helping. The Experiment is not dependent on any formal system of psychology or theology. But it does need the faith that there is a spiritual reality larger and wiser than ourselves, a source of understanding, healing and empowerment, which is waiting for us to invite it into our minds and hearts.

The Light of Christ

Judy Maurer

When I said I didn't understand the image I was given, Arlene giggled. "Don't worry," she said. "My image gave me the answers for all of you."

I knew she wasn't being arrogant. I had been with her in a meditation group for seven years. She is a gentle soul, with a deep concern for the darkest things happening on the planet, so dark I couldn't bear to consider them myself.

Later she wrote up her image:

> *I was gazing into a dark, black cave opening. I knew it contained all grief, loss, chaos, suffering, sin, evil, lies, desolation, and cruelty.*
>
> *I sat comfortably, as if in meditation, on a mossy log. My seat was soft. I was beside a lovely stream, flowers, birds, loveliness all around me. Warming sunlight speckled over me. Without moving, I contemplated the contents in the cave. Then, in a kind of compassion or empathy or desire to 'help,' I said a short prayer.*
>
> *I sensed movement coming up the slope toward the cave, and saw The Mentor striding up behind me.*
>
> *Beyond the peace and beauty I sensed around me, I felt my spirit rise, filled with joy beyond description at The Mentor's coming near. I longed to follow Him, but my arms, legs and body were so heavy and numb, extremely relaxed, that I could not move.*
>
> *The Mentor looked back at me as He passed, smiled and said, 'It's OK. I do this all the time. You can follow me next time, if you're ready.'*
>
> *With all His love, light, power and glory, He entered that source of terror and darkness. I understood that answering my prayer was part of His purpose.*
>
> *The message for all of us was, 'Follow The Mentor.' It gives new meaning to 'Follow Jesus,' and 'Be led by Jesus,' rather than entering that darkness without Him; and the attraction to go with Him when He goes by. The image demonstrates the power and effect, the extreme importance, of prayer.*

Several years ago Diana and John Lampen came to Reedwood Friends in Portland, Oregon, where my husband was a pastor. They were "scholars in residence." They played the tape for the pastoral staff, and then hosted an introductory evening on the Experiment with Light. Many Friends attended, and Diana and John asked if we would like to try it again the following week. We may have seemed a little hesitant at first but we gained courage and agreed. When the practice was over, there was an expectant silence. Then one elderly Friend said, "What an amazing confirmation of God's faithfulness!" Soon afterwards our Light group began as an "official" church activity.

We struggled at first—mostly with the urge to "do it right." I learned that saying to myself, "I have to follow instructions and do it right" became a distraction. It's really a focus on myself and that always gets in the way!

While we kept the invitation open to anyone at the church, we quickly became a close, personal group. After my husband was no longer pastor at Reedwood, Arlene began to host the group at her home. She and others have invited friends and neighbors over the years, and regular attenders now number about eight. The "regulars" include a man who was raised Hindu, a woman who lived in a Buddhist monastery, and another woman who was born in a tiny Mayan village in Guatemala. They now all attend Christian churches.

The meditations have had a profound impact on my life. People have begun saying to me, "you seem like such a calm person." That is new, and is a result of meditating. It has also altered the course of my life.

About five years ago I began working at a social service agency for adults and children with disabilities. The administration was, well, less than stellar. Yet I loved the programs we provided, and for several years I felt I could reliably chart a course above the chaos. Then financial pressures increased, and the chaos became blinding. Accusations and counter-accusations flew. My health deteriorated. For two full weeks, I arrived late every morning because I had to read Romans 12 over and over again, and not leave for work until I was in the mode of its instructions:

> *Bless those who persecute you; bless and do not curse... Do not repay anyone evil for evil. Be careful to do what is right in the eyes of everybody. If it is possible, as far as it depends on you, live at peace with everyone. Do not take revenge, my friends, but leave room for God's wrath, for it is written: "It is mine to avenge; I will repay," says the Lord. On the contrary: "If your enemy is hungry, feed him; if he is thirsty, give him something to drink."*

In this time, my meditation partners were very helpful. I remember telling them about what had happened just that day, and Arlene said, to me, "Now you have the opportunity to be like Christ." I had substituted for her briefly in her job, and I know she had been like Christ there. I could not brush off her instructions.

In my meditations, I often asked God for permission to leave my job. In one image, I was walking up a stoney creek bed in summer in an Oregon forest. The pines were a vivid green, and the smell was sharp and fresh. I could hear birds. Yet the rocks were slippery and the water at my ankles was glacier-cold. With some difficulty, I could have gone to the banks, but the only way to continue through the forest was through the creek. Do I go up the creek, continuing in my task, or do I bail out and go to the banks? I asked. The image changed. I was still walking up the creek, making faster progress, because this time I was wearing thick rubber hip-boots!

I knew exactly what it meant—I needed better personal boundaries. Later I'd often get out of my car in the morning and I say to myself, "hip-boots. Remember your hip-boots." It helped immensely!

A few months later, the dilemma I brought to the light was "Should I be looking for a new job?" I was given an image where I was in a dark room, with rough wood paneling. There was a large picture window, and I realized I was in a house on the Maine coast. It was built above the dunes and I could see the sparse grass of the dunes below, a rickety porch and stairway, and then a path down to the beach and the ocean beyond. I longed to go down to the beach, and feel the sea breeze and see the ocean waves break on the shore, as I had done many times as a child.

But I could not find the door. Despite the picture window, the other walls were cast in darkness. I pressed my hands systematically along the walls, but I could not find the door. Suddenly, I was on the path, the beach and ocean before me, the salt smell vivid, the calls of the seagulls strong in my ear. I still didn't know how I had left the room. The message I took was that I should wait and take no action, because I was not wise enough on my own to know how to leave.

Another week the scene in the creek bed returned. I was in my hip boots, and again I asked, "Should I give up and get on the bank of the creek?" The answer was a firm "No". Yet at the very end of the image, I could hear the distinctive "thwack-thwack" of a helicopter, come to lift me out.

Some of my meditation partners were horrified. "You're going to stay? After all that?" I said yes, and one of them made me promise to be alert for the sound of a helicopter. I admit I almost quit any number of times, but the memory of the images held me back.

Then a few weeks later I was called into my boss' office. Even though I was the only one on staff who had met their revenue goals without going over budget, the board of directors was eliminating my position! I knew I was essentially being fired, but I was relieved and very grateful. My boss felt so badly that he authorized a very generous severance pay. In addition, I was eligible for unemployment compensation. The helicopter had arrived.

I confess that I slept and did nothing for the first few weeks. My physical health began coming back. I realize now that I couldn't have just taken up another job—it had been so stressful that my physical health had to be revived by rest first. God was right—I was not able to see the door on my own.

Later I began applying for other jobs, and offering to volunteer. Nothing came of it, and four months into my six months of unemployment compensation, I began to be anxious. But I was given an image of the floor of a house. On one side of a fireplace and chimney was the dining room, on the other side the living room, much like my childhood home. Yet all the furniture was all at least six feet in the air, swirling around. Then the furniture descended and landed on the floor, precisely in the correct positions.

I understood the relevance to my life immediately. My life felt as if it were all in the air. I rested easily in the knowledge that my future was unfolding as it should. I am now working in an agency doing prevention work in domestic violence; my boss knows the dangers of verbal abuse, and has created an abuse-free zone. It is work-place heaven. The furniture landed in all the right places.

My husband Johan has felt called to be a Quaker missionary in Russia for many, many years. Now, after raising our children but before becoming grandparents, it is his chance. As I write this, he is in the outskirts of Moscow, teaching English and bringing up spiritual issues to begin the work of creating a faith community. I will leave in a few months and join him there.

I have not always been at peace with leaving my job, my friends and my children, now in their early twenties, for Russia. As always, two images have been helpful in this. In one, my husband and I are in a dark Russian forest. It is late winter, when snow begins to leave but first creates icy mud everywhere. The air is cold on my face. Our progress through the woods is slow. I haven't the right kind of boots, and I lose my footing often. At times we have to crawl over logs and piles of debris.

I don't realize that Johan has left my side, but suddenly he appears riding a beautiful black stallion. It is a breathtakingly beautiful animal, and Johan is in high black riding boots and a long black wool coat. I admit he looks very sexy, in a Russian sort of way. He leans down to help me up onto the horse, and when I land in the saddle behind him I realize I fit perfectly on it. I grab onto his waist with both arms and we are off. We fly over the country-side, the horse leaping over anything in our way. It is a joyful, exhilarating ride.

I realize this means that the transition will be difficult, but we will find our way, and then it will be exhilarating to work together. The horse, both massive and beautiful, represents our task together. I begin to look forward to going.

Johan is very firm that he does not see himself as a missionary hero, but is only intent on "discovering what Jesus is already doing in Russia, and joining in."

An image I was given helped me understand. He and I are walking across the unbroken snow. It is a bare, modern scene—there is only flatness, and snow. As he and I walk, I realize a crowd of people is slightly behind us, less than a pace or two away. We are not leading them—we are all walking in the same direction, quietly, with determination. A spare, modern building is on the horizon, with clear blue and white walls, almost industrial-bare in their sheen. We walk toward it, comforted by the knowledge of the silent crowd just a little behind us. Inside there is warmth and light, and Victorian era wood paneling and Persian rugs. Room after room, storey after storey, Johan and I open the doors, and the rooms fill with people. Finally on the fourth floor, the room is an immense amphitheatre, and it is full of people worshiping. We are not leading the worship, however. We are merely watching from the side, Russians leading worship. It is immensely gratifying, and the size of the crowds is, literally, awesome.

The message to me is clear—we will be opening doors. That is all.

It will be difficult to leave my meditation group to go to Russia. We have been together through many crises and triumphs, filling each other in every week. And who would not miss someone like Arlene? While my dilemmas, and therefore my images, are about my life—recalcitrant teens, difficult bosses, etc, —her images are universal. Here's another one she wrote up. The focus she took into meditation that day was "I am beginning to dislike some people. What about that?"

> *The image was of a pink crayon, in a corner of a dark space, a small child's hand writing on a little tablet. Next to it was a yellow legal pad with an adult's handwriting on it. Other forms of written text*

appeared: a tapestry with a nice border and Persian script; a computer screen full of text; a page of a book. There were other formats of texts, and scripts of all languages and time periods. Each form of text faded as the next took shape or appeared in different planes. The series speeded up, then ended abruptly.

I understood the common meaning of all these texts: "Someone disliked someone else."

The Mentor's message in words to me was, "I've heard it all and I don't want to hear more."

Since the beginning of history, dislike has run like a current through humanity. This message expressed both The Mentor's sorrow at the perverse "dislike/hate" tendency, as well as His will being that we stop it. On the spectrum of violence, dislike is a rung on hate's ladder.

I recalled how The Mentor's directions to me have often been "Love and be loving," in many contexts and meditations. This requires my faith and Christ-love entering me like a current, flowing into the relationship and the circumstance. Having "a pure heart" is part of it. This is my special prayer, and where I find Reverence for Life to be. Anything less is the opposite way, not Christ-Spirit's "I am the Way and the Life."

The Meeting

Cynthia Jones

I dove into the meeting like an intense love affair. I opened my heart unashamedly. I wept. I felt joy. I was awakened and renewed. I made a private spiritual dance with each person. And in the end I still wondered if I was OK.

I had embraced death as an indifferent stage of life. I sit at the feet of my ageless elders and they prepare me to live longer. I came in cloaked and I stand naked and exposed; the light burns my eyes.

I am seeking. First with each member. "Are you my mother, are you my mother?" like the chick that hatched from the displaced egg. And next I wonder "Will you love me too?" not realizing I wear my mother on my sleeve. I am ashamed to ask and afraid to know. The condition of approval is pending. And this is a new territory for me. I have never stood on this ground before. I have never been so grounded. I am accustomed to floating, fleeing, and there is nowhere to hide—no need.

I am in a crazy love affair with this meeting. Crazy like I never knew love before. Crazy like I am trusting in spite of myself and there is no betrayal under this light. It is uneasy like flying without the net.

I dare. I am coming up for air from that greedy lustful plunge. I am hungry and wanting more and wanting to run and wanting more and wanting to distance myself from being caught loving.

I am deepening my capacity for love and it makes me feel vulnerable...and if I blink, very much alone. Why is that?

I disintegrate in the light and am formed again, luminous body, and I feel so separate.

Consider—how I need to act.

Hold this—all of it, as you grow into your skin.

[Written during an Experiment with Light practice on "the group", 28.2.2007]

Experiment With Light and Prayer

Marcelle Martin

I was introduced to Experiment with Light by JoAnn Seaver, who had visited a Light group in England and came back to Philadelphia eager to share the practice with local Friends. For many years I had intensively practiced another form of meditation also designed to help one directly face the fears and complex emotions underlying the difficult situations in one's life. I was interested to learn about Experiment with Light and how this meditation practice had been connected to the experience of early Friends. I joined JoAnn's exploratory group, committing to a four week experience together. Once a week we listened to the recorded voices of British Friends inviting us to focus on something in our lives about which we felt discomfort.

"Let the Light show you what's really going on in your life," Diana Lampen's voice suggested on the tapes.

The first few times I did the Experiment with Light meditations, I received a stream of images that seemed rather fanciful. With some embarrassment, I shared those images with the members of my small group, who listened with quiet attention. When I was at home afterwards, especially while walking up the dark narrow staircase to my third-floor bedroom, I had a gentle sense of something shining in and around me. It wasn't visible with my eyes; I perceived in some other way, perhaps with my heart. I wasn't sure if this light was heightened in me by the meditation, or by the loving, nonjudgmental attention of the Friends who had listened to me share my images. In any case, it was clear I was encountering the Light, so I returned for subsequent sessions.

At that time I was suffering from serious chronic fatigue. The Light Group that formed after the initial exploration met at a location difficult for me to get to, so I did not become a regular member. I did, however, attend occasionally, and whenever I did, I was aware of an intensified experience of the Light, both during the meditations and afterwards. Over the following years, the members of that group formed deep spiritual bonds. When I visited them, the feeling of the Presence was very strong and I had the experience of being quickly gathered, as if we were in a deep meeting for worship. One evening when we met, I had the image that we were sitting together experiencing a spiritual radiation, as from a warm fire on a cold night.

Once while doing the Experiment with Light, I was so fatigued that I did the meditation lying down on a meetinghouse bench. I paid attention to the heavy weight I felt in my life, in particular as it related to my chronic fatigue, and asked the Light to give me a deeper understanding of what was going on. I gradually found myself thinking about a U.S. soldier who had been held captive in Iraq after the other soldiers in her unit were killed. She had sustained several broken bones, including a broken spine, and other injuries, both physical and psychological. During my meditation I found myself thinking of her need to stay very still for a long time in order for her broken spine and other injuries to heal. Some words came to me with a certain clarity and compassion.

"Some things take a long time to heal."

Then I realized that the injured soldier's story had come so strongly into my mind during the meditation as a metaphor for my own condition. This image brought more understanding of my situation—I was healing from multiple serious injuries, not only physical but also psychological. Being very still was required for healing—hence, the chronic fatigue actually served the helpful function of keeping me still much more than I would have been inclined to be. Most of all, I experienced a sense of compassion for myself. Since then I have many times returned to the memory of that meditation. As I remember it now, I have a sense that the compassionate understanding I'd received had a divine source. I feel I was companioned in that meditation by God. It was an experience of prayer.

There are many forms of prayer. Traditional Christian prayers have stressed talking to God—to thank, praise, confess, or ask for help for oneself or others. Countless prayers of this kind have been written down, many of them used in church liturgies or published in prayer books; often they are read aloud, recited from memory, or repeated inwardly. For many, the word "prayer" is associated with these forms. However, there are other ways to pray. For me, prayer is any communication or communion with the Divine, or even any attempt to be aware of the Divine. I think of the Divine as ultimate Reality, so attempting to be fully present to reality is also prayer. Quakers stress the prayer of listening for divine guidance, a prayer that may not contain any words at all, even inwardly. Prayer can simply be the act or intention of being receptive to the Divine, not only to divine guidance, but to illumination, energy, healing, and the gradual process of union. When early Quakers wrote of their experiences in worship, they wrote of waiting in silence, emptying their minds of themselves and their own thoughts until they experienced a Presence among them. They described the awesome Power of the Lord which they often felt and which transformed them and their lives. Waiting for and being receptive to that Presence and Power is prayer.

The Light that early Friends spoke of was the Light of Christ Within, the same Light that "lighteth every man that comes into the world." (John 1:9) And every woman, too, I want to add. Sometimes in my own encounters with the Light—while doing the Experiment with Light, in prayer, and in spontaneous experiences—I have the sense that this is the same Light that was in Jesus. At other times, this Light seems to have a more universal aspect. Much of the time I don't have any particular sense of light at all, inner or outer. Sometimes I gain a subtle awareness of something that had been obscure before. At other times, I feel like I am touched by a love or wisdom or peace that seems to be an expression of who I am in my best potential. A Hindu might think of this Light as Kundalini Shakti. It is not necessary to be a Christian, or a Quaker, or even a person who believes in God in order to practice Experiment With Light and receive illumination, release, understanding, or healing. When speculating on the source of the illumination that comes in this practice, I sometimes think about the wisdom that created my body out of a single cell and which continually monitors all of the countless delicate functions necessary to maintain it now. As I practice the Experiment With Light meditation, I open to that amazing wisdom which is beyond my conscious mind, a wisdom that understands all the most intricate workings of my body, mind, and spirit. Perhaps its source is what is called God.

Rex Ambler's personal story, which he recounts in *Light to Live By*, shows how, as we practice the meditation over time, our relationship with the Light and our understanding of it changes and grows. As we experience more frequently and directly the Mystery which shapes and wishes to guide our lives in partnership with us, our theology gradually develops along new lines. But no particular theological belief system is required in order to practice the meditation or benefit from it. As George Fox insisted, it was not necessary to take his word about the operation of the Light within; the important thing was to try it and experience it for ourselves.

Rex Ambler and Diana Lampen came to teach Experiment With Light at a weeklong course at Pendle Hill in 2003. A part-time faculty member at Pendle Hill, I accepted the role of "spiritual nurturer" for course participants. I listened to many people share experiences they'd had during their meditations—sometimes little insights, sometimes big ones. When they spoke, their faces seemed to shine with light. Sharing with one's small group usually brought greater understanding. One woman present had been regularly practicing the Experiment with Light meditations for months already, experiencing them as a form of prayer, and came to Pendle Hill with an openness to a more profound level of experience. That week she did have a significant spiritual opening during one of her meditations—the sort of experience that tends to leave one in a new state of understanding about life, but at first somewhat disoriented. She identified with a passage by Margaret Fell that Rex had quoted, about letting the Light rip one up and leave one bare.

Generally, our meditations bring up no more than we can handle. Usually we receive subtle and gentle insights, but sometimes we receive stark clarity about realities we have been denying, including the need to make major changes in our lives. Descriptions of how the early Friends experienced the Light reflect awesome, life-changing encounters. One of the chapters in Hugh Barbour's book, *The Quakers in Puritan England*, is entitled "The Power and Terror of the Light." Early Friends understood that the Light was asking them to make radical changes in the way they lived, changes that made them different from others in their society and often brought mockery and even persecution upon them. The Light shook the lives and beliefs of those seventeenth century Friends to the foundations. They had such powerful encounters with the Light in no small measure because of the intensity of their common desire to know and do God's will. The divine Power they experienced is what made Quakers quake in 1652, and today it still causes Friends to quake when we open ourselves to it in a radical way, as I have witnessed. I believe that though it may shake us, the Light shows us no more than we can handle at any given time, in the company of Friends.

In my own meditations at Pendle Hill that week, I was shown that I was being called to enter into a different kind of teaching role, one that was more about being and about serving than about mastering and explaining information. I was also given the insight that it would be good for me to come to Pendle Hill as a resident student. Then, in the wee hours of the last night of the course, I had an unusual experience. I was awakened with a sense of a light hovering over me, particularly over my abdomen. This light had a question for me.

"Will you serve me?"

"Of course, I'm always trying to serve you," I responded sleepily in my mind, not fully awake to what was happening. Then I sensed that this was a feeble and certainly inadequate response to "Will you serve me?"

To wake myself up to what was being asked of me and to take it as seriously as possible, I got out of my bed and down on my knees. I did not know exactly how I was being asked to serve, but it had something to do with sharing the Experiment With Light in the United States, and particularly at Pendle Hill.

"Yes, I'll serve you," I said as whole-heartedly as I knew, making a commitment. It was a prayer: communication and communion with something Divine.

I've received many layers of understanding about the meaning of that night-time experience. First, it revealed something lukewarm in my general attitude toward the Light. In practicing the meditation, and in my other prayers as well, I had generally been turning to the Light because I want to be served by it in some way: "Help me understand this, help me fix this, show me the way, heal this and that."

The Light loves us and wants to serve us, in fact is constantly serving us whether we ask or not, and is delighted when we choose to take fuller advantage of the gifts available to us by consciously seeking its assistance. Yet, as my relationship with the Light has grown, I have become more aware that I am also invited to love the Light. George Fox said, "Thou who lovest the Light, here is thy teacher...."

Underlying my whole life is the question asked by the Light that night, "Will you serve me?" Repeatedly I am given the opportunity to serve God—or to serve something else. Again and again I find myself in a sleepy state and have to choose to wake up to a more conscious way to love the Light and serve divine purposes, instead of lesser ones.

Pendle Hill invited Rex to come back and teach his course again soon; however, because of the high cost of airfares, they asked him to choose an assistant from this side of the ocean. He invited me. This seemed a way I was meant to serve the Light, and I agreed. I prepared by facilitating two four-week Experiment With Light courses, one at my own meeting and another at a nearby meeting. Using *Light to Live By* as our text, we practiced several versions of the meditation. At the end of each course, one or more Light Groups were formed in the meetings.

By the time Rex returned to Pendle Hill in February 2005 to teach his course again, I was enrolled as a resident student at Pendle Hill. While doing the meditation one day during that course, I focused on the blocked feeling I had about my writing. I had come to Pendle Hill planning to work on a particular project, but was not feeling any life in it. Instead, ideas for other projects had more energy, including a nudge to write a pamphlet about prayer. I didn't know if this was a leading, however. Maybe I was just distracting myself.

In the meditation, I invited the Light to illuminate what was really going on with my writing block. An image came to me of a woman lying face down in the snow with her hands tied together behind her back, an early Quaker woman in colonial New England. For a couple of years I had been devoting my summers to writing about women with a sense of divine mission. I had focused one summer on reading and writing about Elizabeth Hooton, the first Quaker woman minister, but I had gotten stuck. It was hard to tell Elizabeth's story without also recounting the story of George Fox and explaining the birth of Quakerism. As I tried to write about Quakerism, I'd felt I needed to understand the historical context better, and had started reading about English history, the Protestant Reformation, and Puritanism. By the time that summer was over, I hadn't gotten very far in the life of Elizabeth Hooton, and the following summer I took up another woman's story.

Elizabeth had been one of many punished in Massachusetts under the harsh Puritan "Cart and Tail Law." It involved stripping Quakers to the waist, tying them to the back of a cart, and whipping them. Then the cart pulled them to the next village, where they were whipped again, and so on until they were out of the colony, where they were left in the wilderness. Elizabeth was a persistent and hardy soul who returned to New England and was punished under the Cart and Tail law several times. Once when she and her companion were left in a frozen wilderness, they survived by following wolf prints in the snow.

My meditation had given me an image of a solitary Quaker woman face down in the snow. All that came in response to the later prompts of the meditation was a clearer focus on her bound hands. How did this image reflect my condition in relation to my writing? Later that day, I tried to gain more understanding by putting my body in the physical position of the woman in my image. When I imagined pulling my hands apart, the loop of strong rope around them did not give.

In meeting for worship the next morning, I saw the image of the bound hands. Again I imagined pulling the hands apart, straining against the rope, but still they would not come free. I offered this image and the situation it represented up to God and let it go. Later in worship, the image of the bound hands came again. This time, the hands did not pull against the rope. Instead, I saw them press themselves together, in a gesture of prayer. Then they slid easily out of the loop that had been binding them.

"Ah, I need to pray about it," I said to myself.

In prayer, it seemed that the Light was showing me I needed to write about prayer: that was the project I should take up.

Of course, the image had other layers of meaning as well. It reflected deep culturally embedded fears about the consequences of expressing a radical faith—consequences experienced in brutal ways by the first Quaker Publishers of Truth. What if I were as persistently outspoken as Elizabeth Hooton? Would I, too, be beaten in some way and left cold and alone? In this and in other images given in meditation, I sensed that it was not just personal fears and injuries that were being brought into the Light for healing, but also something beyond myself, something archetypal and historical, wounds in the collective unconscious related to patriarchal suppression of women, denial of direct experience of the divine, and muffling of the prophetic voice. Those fears and frozen energies required prayer, and not just solitary prayer.

One evening soon after the workshop, at Pendle Hill's Sunday night Meeting for Prayer and Healing, I sat down on the chair inside the square of benches and asked for prayer for what was blocking me in my writing. Several Friends came over and laid hands on me, while others prayed from their seats. One Friend prayed out loud. Then I had an image of an eagle flying out of my throat with a loud cry, as though something blocked in my voice had been liberated. The eagle flew straight up into the air.

The release that came in this time of communal prayer, along with the image of the bound hands being released by coming together in prayer, gave me the necessary focus for my writing at that time.

During my two terms as a resident student at Pendle Hill, I wrote a couple of drafts of what would become my Pendle Hill pamphlet, *Holding One Another in the Light*. It was published just a year after the Experiment With Light workshop in which I'd seen the woman with bound hands.

The summer after my pamphlet was published, I returned again to writing about Elizabeth Hooton, but at the same time I also wrote about Mary Dyer, Mary Fisher, Mary Penington, and Margaret Fell, fellow seventeenth-century Quaker women. In the book I am still writing, Elizabeth is now no longer a suffering solitary figure alone in the wilderness, as she'd been in my image, but part of a vibrant network of Quaker ministers (male as well as female) who loved and supported each other in adversity.

As my examples illustrate, the Experiment With Light meditation is a form of prayer for me. My practice of the Experiment with Light is part of a multi-faceted relationship with the Divine. My experiences in the meditation provide images and information that I bring to other kinds of prayer and worship. Ultimately, we take up spiritual practices such as meditation, regular prayer, and meeting for worship in order to help us focus on God and create habits of relationship that more and more frequently and spontaneously become our practice in all the moments of our lives. JoAnn Seaver wrote to me out of her many years of experience with the Light Group she started in Philadelphia: "I think Experiment with Light and the meeting for worship, along with individual prayer—without getting into the distinctions among the three—are mutually reinforcing. They are three beneficial practices in relating to the divine reality beyond our notions, and expressing in our lives God's hope for us. Practice, practice, practice."

Discernment and Peace Making

Helene Pollock

I have always wanted my activism to be grounded in my spiritual life. At the same time, I have resisted a spirituality that is cut off from the world of politics and action. A member of the baby-boomer generation, my worldview has been shaped by the civil rights movement, the Viet Nam war, and the feminist and gay-rights movements. Through the years I have seen many different kinds of political challenges.

One of my clearest political recollections is of the weeks immediately preceding the U.S. invasion of Iraq, in 2003. It was a time of real intensity, politically. At that precise moment of impending doom, as war clouds loomed on the horizon, a workshop on the Experiment with Light had been scheduled at Pendle Hill, a Quaker study center near Philadelphia.[1] Diana Lampen and Rex Ambler had agreed to lead the workshop.

My friend JoAnn Seaver and I had started a Light Group in JoAnn's home about a year prior to the workshop. The group was going well. We signed up for the workshop in an attitude of hopefulness.

Arriving at Pendle Hill, I carried with me vivid images of the massive anti-war protest in New York City—300,000 to 400,000 strong—that I had participated in two weeks prior. It was a global day of protest: February 15, 2003. Six to ten million people in sixty countries demonstrated against the impending invasion.[2] Three million people gathered in Rome for the largest anti-war rally in history.[3] People were not accepting George Bush's supposed justification for "regime change" in Iraq.[4] There was profound skepticism about the scenario that was being constructed about Iraq's alleged weapons of mass destruction. People weren't falling for the innuendoes about Saddam Hussein's ties with al-Qaeda. Since then, the skepticism of world opinion has proved to be justified. The alleged weapons of mass destruction for which the US and coalition partners invaded have never been found, nor has evidence of an operational or collaborative relationship between Saddam Hussein and al-Qaeda.

[1] The actual dates of the workshop were March 3-7, 2003.

[2] According to a BBC News estimate.

[3] According to the *2004 Guinness Book of World Records*.

[4] A 2003 Gallup poll covering 41 countries claimed that less than 10% would support an invasion of Iraq without UN sanction and that half would not support an invasion under any circumstances.

At the workshop, there was a mood of cataclysmic impotence. How would Diana and Rex address the proverbial "elephant in the living room"? Would the sinking sensation be acknowledged – the premonition that war was inevitable, in spite of the protests?

Diana and Rex made it clear that they had no intention to sidestep reality. After giving us a basic grounding in the rationale and methodology for the Experiment with Light, they scheduled an extended meditation on "the world," in complete silence. By then the group had become sufficiently familiar with the method to do the meditation without using the spoken prompts. There in the silence, in total honesty, we were challenged to come face to face with the state of our world. We had our physical eyes closed, but our inner eyes were wide open to the world. We gazed at reality unblinkingly, together.

I remember a distinct sense of deepening. I remember being grateful for not being alone. In a state of naked honesty, it came to me beyond all doubt I was truly longing for something new. That certainty was encouraging, even though no answer was in sight.

I waited and waited. Eventually it came to me that I am the type of person who tends to see issues in terms of individual people. Could that be a starting point? I pondered that possibility for some time. Finally, after a long struggle, an answer came. Unsteadily, yet with a sense of relief, I welcomed it. As we joined hands at the end of the meditation, I remember feeling grateful, because I knew what I needed to do.

As soon as I got home, I went to see Linda Panetta of the School of the Americas Watch.[5] Linda had recently returned from a trip to Iraq, and had shared her beautiful photos of Iraqi people at an ecumenical peace event. I explained my plan, and she immediately agreed. She helped me figure out how to transfer three of her photos of people in Iraq on to three pieces of white cloth that were approximately one foot square. Under each photo I wrote in bold marker: MY FAMILY IN IRAQ.

It wasn't long before the dreaded day came. About two weeks after the workshop, on March 20, the US launched its nearly unilateral invasion of Iraq, with military support from small contingents from Great Britain, Australia, Denmark and Poland. The invasion took place with great whoopla. The media tried to create the impression of a swiftly efficient triumph without serious consequences. Of course, people around me were sick at heart.

[5] http://www.soaw.org/

"My family in Iraq"

The woman in the middle of the upper picture lost her husband (whose picture she is holding) when he was killed by a pre-emptive bombing strike in Basra just prior to the "official" start of the war.

Immediately after hearing about the invasion, with an attitude of certainty, I pinned one of the cloths to my back. My intention was to wear one of the cloths morning, noon and night, everywhere I went, as a symbol of my identity in relationship to the war.

The next morning as I was preparing to wear one of the cloths to work, I experienced some trepidation. My office was located directly across the hall from the office of the President of the College. While we had an informal dress code in the office, the atmosphere was appropriately professional. I arrived at the office with a cloth on my back, and nothing happened. I continued wearing a cloth each day, rotating the pictures depending on my mood. People didn't say anything.

The President of the College at the time was Thomas R. Tritton, a Quaker who had been a conscientious objector during the Viet Nam war. He eventually asked if I was wearing the cloths as an individual decision or as part of a group. When I told him that I was the only one doing this he said nothing more. With some caution, I wore a cloth on my back at the board meeting, without consulting the President ahead of time. Neither he nor anyone else said anything.

There was one person who spoke about the cloths – a manual laborer. He was a controversial person, known as a trouble-maker in his department. He came up to me one day with what appeared to be a sincere question about how I happened to have relatives in Iraq. I tried to explain to him that it was a symbolic picture, but he seemed to not understand. He came back to me on other occasions, inquiring about my relatives in Iraq. To this day I am not sure whether he was simply being literalistic, or whether he was knowingly confronting me with a deeply ironic question.

In retrospect, I see my decision to wear the cloths as representing a mild challenge to the behavioral norms of the office. To talk openly about the war (outside of one-on-one private conversations) would have been very unnatural, and it probably would have been contentious. So I was not surprised when people studiously ignored the cloths.

Since 2003, the political climate has evolved – globally, nationally, and in my office. I continue to be aware of the political realities at my job, in the Religious Society of Friends, and elsewhere, as I take note of the norms governing political discourse. It is my intention to be as open as possible to any political risk that I may be called to undertake.

Another participant in the Pendle Hill event was Tom Fox, whose experience with the Experiment with Light is described by Diana earlier.[6] Tom didn't stand out during the Pendle Hill workshop in any particular way. But he was later to become known to millions when he was kidnapped and killed in Iraq while serving as a member of the Christian Peacemaker Teams.

Tom Fox had a deep spiritual core. He included the words "inner light" on his email address. He also put them on his license plate. But that didn't mean that he found it easy to meditate. He was first introduced to the Experiment with Light in 2001, at a workshop at Guilford College, but it took some months of practice for him to be able to use the meditation productively.

About a year after Tom's introduction to the Experiment with Light, he faced a major spiritual turning point when the events of September 11, 2001, occurred. September 11 became a touchstone for subsequent decisions he would make. Drawing on images of his inner landscape, Tom describes his experience of September 11 in these words:

> As I was watching the events in New York City and Washington, I had a strong sense of one of the—for lack of a better word— "visions" that the founder of Quakerism, George Fox, experienced... It was my clear experience that day that we were being drawn deeper into the ocean of darkness and were creating more distance between ourselves and the infinite love of God.

During a guided meditation several months later (was it during a Light Group or in some other setting?) Tom received a strong image of the scales of justice, along with an inner certainty about the need for people to make a conscious choice for peace or war.

Tom began searching for a Christian group that was committed to nonviolence. He had become clear about his commitment to Jesus twenty years earlier when an elderly Friend delivered this simple message during worship: "I feel that in all things we need to keep to Jesus."

Shortly before registering for the workshop with Rex and Diana, Tom found the Christian Peacemaker Teams on the internet. After the workshop, he continued his explorations of CPT in earnest. He submitted his application on September 11, 2003, offering himself for full-time service with them at a later time. He spent the summers of 2003 and 2004 working at a Quaker summer camp. His commitment to working with young people was central

[6] See page 26

to his sense of service. He completed CPT's training program immediately after camp ended in 2004. He left for Iraq on September 11, 2004.

Tom's CPT work in Iraq involved living in solidarity with ordinary people and supporting Iraqi peace initiatives. A fellow team member described Tom as "a calm, centered Quaker who began each day before dawn on the roof of our apartment building doing yoga and meditating." One time when the team was facing a difficult decision Tom suggested that they spend time in silence so that people could search their hearts, listening carefully to the Spirit. After doing so, the team came to unity much more easily than they would have predicted.[7]

Tom's spirituality had its foundation in a process of focusing on reality. He was committed to seeing the world *as it really is*. This was often a painful, disorienting experience for him—like being "in the middle of nowhere." [8]

> How do I stay with the pain and suffering and not be overwhelmed? How do I resist the welling up of rage towards the perpetrators of violence? How do I keep from disconnecting from or becoming numb to the pain?
>
> After eight months with Christian Peacemaker Teams… I have to struggle harder and harder each day against my desire to move away or become numb. Simply staying with the pain of others doesn't seem to create any healing or transformation. Yet there seems to be no other first step into the realm of compassion than to not step away.
>
> [In the words of Pema Chodron] "Becoming intimate with the queasy feeling of being in the middle of nowhere makes our hearts more tender. When we are brave enough to stay in the nowhere place then compassion arises spontaneously."
>
> Being in the middle of nowhere really does create a very queasy feeling and yet so many spiritual teachers say it is the only authentic place to be. Not staking out any ground for myself creates the possibility of standing with anyone. The middle of nowhere is the one place where compassion can be discovered. The constant challenge is recognizing that my true country of origin is in the middle of nowhere.

In November of 2005, after he had been with CPT for about two years, Tom Fox was kidnapped along with three other CPT members. Their lives were threatened if all Iraqi detainees were not immediately released. Messages of support came in from around the world, including many from the Muslim community. On March 10, 2006, Tom Fox's body was recovered in

[7] From a eulogy for Tom Fox by Bob Holmes, http://www.cpt.org/memorial/tomfox/eulogies.htm

[8] "No Words" From the Weblog of Tom Fox. p. 8-9. *Friends Journal*, May 2006

Baghdad. On March 23, his three fellow peacemakers were rescued by multinational forces without a shot being fired.

My friend JoAnn Seaver, a retired educator in her 70s and a lifelong activist, first heard about the Experiment with Light when she read about it in Friends Journal. I helped make arrangements for her to meet the Lampens and Rex Ambler during a trip she took to England. She had a powerful experience of her first Light Group in Rex Ambler's living room. On her return, she and I established a Light Group in Philadelphia. After the group had been going for about a year, she and I attended the Pendle Hill workshop led by Diana and Rex.

Some time after the workshop, one evening when JoAnn was participating in a Light Group meditation, the words came to her: *"Get out on the street."* JoAnn was not clear about the actual implications of the words, but they carried the force of truth, so she took them seriously and they stayed with her. She trusted that "further instructions" would be forthcoming.

A few months later there was a serious gang fight in JoAnn's neighborhood, outside a public comprehensive high school of 1400 students.[9] Notoriously chaotic and chronically under-funded, one-quarter of its students were in special education. During this particular fight a boy was shot. He survived, but the community was shaken.

JoAnn was on the board of a small Kindergarten-to-8th-grade Friends School located near the high school. When the fight and shooting occurred, the board became concerned not only for the Friends' School students (since their bus stop was near the high school), but also for the staff and the youth of the high school.

The community took action. Over a thousand African-American men joined together, circling the high school in prayer. This led to the formation of the Germantown Clergy Initiative, to sustain the concern. Their first project was a "safe corridor," a presence on the streets before and after school. Leaders of the initiative were pastors of local African-American congregations.

[9] In the U.S. context, a "comprehensive" high school means a "non-selective" school which is open to students who were not accepted or did not apply to the various public or private high schools that have a special academic or vocational focus.

JoAnn felt drawn to join the safe corridor initiative. She remembered the call to *"get out on the street"* and recognized that here was the opportunity to do just that. So she joined the safe corridor initiative. She began volunteering, doing two 45-minute "shifts," before and after school, one day each week. She also started attending weekly planning meetings of the Germantown Clergy Initiative. This is how she describes the work:

> The first year, we gathered at a storefront church and huddled for a prayer before going out. Then we went out as partners, carrying a walkie talkie with which to call the police if necessary. But our job wasn't primarily to call the police; it was to hold the students in prayer and to greet them warmly.
>
> I saw how beautiful the kids were. As they relaxed, they were clearly just high school kids. It took a year and a half before they could trust us enough to say 'good morning' back to us. When that first happened, it was a wonderful day. Now it's commonplace.
>
> We have changed the climate on the street. Fights still happen, but it's a different atmosphere. We made it clear that we cared about the kids. The police response changed; it became more measured. At times there has been violence. Some students have run to the men for protection. The men began mentoring the boys during school every Wednesday; they took the kids on trips to colleges.
>
> Because of our steadfastness – in all kinds of weather – we managed to gain credibility with the students, with the community, and with the school district, in advocating for the school. We became advocates for the school. We raised money for the school. We started a parent center and sponsored a 'restorative practice' workshop for teachers. We were represented on the selection committee for the new principal.

After four years with the safe corridor initiative, JoAnn and her fellow volunteers are still going strong. And she is still faithful to the call that came to her in the Light Group to "*get out on the street.*" Over the years she has gotten a sense of what those words mean. This is how she explains it:

> "When you're on the street, you see people face to face. Then it's easy to work on their behalf. You have to meet the people you're called to support, because the energy is love; the satisfaction is love."

Inspired by the example of Tom Fox and JoAnn Seaver, as well as many others, I continue to evolve in my understanding of the relationship between spirituality and activism. Each day I spend considerable time in prayer.

This includes going through the basic steps of the Experiment with Light meditation—doing a "scan" of my life and the wider world to see what makes me uncomfortable, focusing, waiting for an answer, opening myself to any new Light that is given, and writing in my journal.

The motivation underlying everything—at the core of my being—is a longing to relate to God. As I wrote recently in my journal:

> I realize that God's love is a perfect fit for the empty abyss in my soul. God and I are a perfect fit for each other. The empowerment comes from a realization that *I can change*, as God empowers me to do so. I can let go of my will, my assumptions. God can transform my needs when I surrender my will. I am accepting God as God, more and more fully, and allowing that experience to be central.

The times when I receive specific guidance are wonderful. There were the cloth pictures of "My family in Iraq." And there was another time when I became aware that I needed to attend a rally for immigration rights, while also developing closer ties to immigrant families in my community. That was after hearing the words "Stand up!" during prayer one day, and writing these words in my journal:

> I need to open up much more, to make room for what has been shut out and excluded – parts of myself, parts of the human experience, concrete human beings who are waiting, yearning, hungry for the very things they brought to Jesus, and found in Him. In the emptiness I find what was always there, but lost to my awareness. Jesus shakes things up to make that possible.

There have been times of deep inner pain. I can identify with what Tom Fox called "the middle of nowhere." The experience of disorientation has been nearly overwhelming at times.

It takes real courage to meditate unblinkingly on the world before moving to action, being committed to a discernment process that is essentially *not* results-oriented. This requires a complete commitment—which is for me a total attitude of submission to God—in order to be truly *open* to the will of God, not insisting on or even hoping for any specific outcome. I have found that this radical openness to God and to reality helps me put spirituality and activism in balance. For me this radical openness has become a reliable foundation for peacemaking.

Introducing Experiment with Light to Young People

Kerstin Backman

Seven years ago I was given an opportunity to introduce Experiment with Light to teenagers. This has given a new sense of purpose to my last couple of years as a grammar school teacher. Let me tell you how it came about.

I teach English and Latin at an upper secondary school just north of Stockholm, Sweden. My school is organised quite differently from other Swedish schools; it uses the American style where a student meets a new group with every course he takes and doesn't get to know many other students (or teachers) particularly well. Some seven years ago the school health staff initiated "Life Enjoyment Day" (sic!) for all second-year students. The plan was to give the students a rest from all the academics and also to show them other sources of wisdom. The programme still continues and the Day starts with a captivating lecture and ends with some stand-up comedy. In between the students attend two one-hour workshops of their choice. The workshops vary between learning Salsa, talking about drug dangers, or hearing about Ayurveda.

When the first "L E Day" had happened, I realised that Experiment with Light in one form or another belonged there. I approached the responsible persons, offering a programme called "Discover Silence" for the year ahead. My offer was accepted, if somewhat hesitatingly. Later everybody was pleasantly surprised to find that "Discover Silence" had been the first workshop to be fully booked. I had presented it in writing as a way of learning to see silence as a resource rather than a threat. The students said that they had realised that silence had become a rare commodity in their lives and had been intrigued by my presentation.

The first session (in 2000) was very different from the one I carried out in April this year (2007), because, basing this on what the students tell me in the final round, I always think of ways of improving the workshop, mainly (as it turns out) the introduction. To begin with, I didn't realise how difficult it was for the students to understand what I meant by "letting your thoughts disappear". I was also so anxious not to pry into their experiences that I refrained from asking them anything whatsoever afterwards. But their nonplussed faces as they left worried me, so the following year I told them I was pleased that so many chose "Discover Silence", but wondered whether I had cheated them and had better stop. I didn't get any useful answers then, but during the final stand-up show a girl came up to me and whispered, "Don't stop! I got such a kick out of it, afterwards."

Today and until further notice, my two one-hour workshops look like this:

- Not more than 12 participants
- A room in a distant corner of the school, not altogether sound-proof, but okay
- Room furnished with chairs in a round (comfortable chairs taken from the adjacent computer room)
- The students are 17 years old. Both boys and girls participate. They don't necessarily know each other and I don't know them, except a few who come to my English or Latin. I explain that in order for us all to feel comfortable, I will ask them to sit next to somebody they don't know and introduce themselves and say what attracted them to this workshop. I then ask them to share the same information to the whole group.
- I then introduce the meditation. Sometimes, as I try to do it without a manuscript, parts get left out, but the following is what I try to get across:

  "Life can easily turn into a race, a competition or a happening demanding more and more action. Many are embarrassed by a few moments' silence.

  As a matter of fact – as I see it – we actually need the silent pauses. Music wouldn't be music without the pauses. And it's the same with us. The pauses and the silence become a time for processing our everyday impressions. In the processing, what we think and feel emerges more clearly. It becomes easier for us to stand up for who we are.

  At the same time the pauses and the silence give us an opportunity to digest what somebody else has said or shown. If somebody around us is unhappy, we can notice it, reflect on it and act on it.

  But in order for this to work, in order to make the most of this silence, you need to feel comfortable with it, and know how to use it. There are loads of methods. This is just one. It is based on the conviction that a human being does not exclusively consist of brains. Feelings, experiences, needs, memories etc – together with thoughts – contribute to accumulating a bank of wisdom on the inside. When you want to access this bank account, however, thinking is not enough. Most school work amounts to so much

> *thinking, and you mustn't think I am against it. But today we'll practise heeding the rest!*
>
> *I will give you seven short instructions, leaving five minutes' silence between each. Follow the instructions as best you can. Close your eyes to avoid wondering what the others are thinking about you. Afterwards I'll ask you to share how you felt about the silence. Remember that you don't have to tell us the actual contents of your experience."*

This year, the introduction raised a few interesting questions, like: "You have told us about accessing the bank account, but how do you deposit resources there?" (Quick thinking! "By living" was all I could come up with.) Another boy said he couldn't possibly imagine himself not thinking, so I let the whole group practise before the meditation:

- Close your eyes
- Be in your head and notice what it feels like
- Be in your chest and notice what it feels like
- Notice any difference?

The answer was yes and I advised them to recur to this exercise whenever they felt like giggling or "thinking". I think this little preparation might explain why the same boy said afterwards: "I think I became a Christian. I've been thinking about it but I haven't been able to say that I believe in God." Now it had become possible. I was elated.

Thus, after the meditation I ask them to share with the same person as before what the meditation has meant to them, and then again with the whole group. The responses are usually not as dramatic as the examples above ("a kick" and "God") and range from "Nothing in particular" over "It was difficult to stop thinking" to "It was relaxing". I also give them a small piece of paper with the instructions on it, and a microscopic www.kvakare.se at the foot.

The actual meditation I have modified somewhat, to suit the sixty-minute format and to avoid elements that might put a 17-year-old secular Swede off. In the most recent version I even eliminated the word "the Light" in order to facilitate the participants' discovery of their inner processes. The previous group had told me that it wasn't obvious what "The Light" meant. So here goes:

DISCOVER SILENCE
(5 MINUTES' SILENCE AFTER EVERY INSTRUCTION)

1) Be still. Sit comfortably. Relax and feel how you become heavy. Let your thoughts disappear. Pay attention to your breathing. Be still.

2) Wait. Prepare yourself for what might appear. Close your eyes and pay attention to what is going on inside you. Wait.

3) Pay attention. Let your inside ["The Light"] show you what is important, or tough, just now. Pay attention.

4) Be prepared to see things in a new light.

5) Acknowledge that which appears. Continue to wait. Acknowledge.

6) Look back on what has appeared in the silence. Reflect on its meaning for you.

7) When you feel ready, open your eyes and finish the session. Wait for all the others to return.

Now you know about my speed version of Experiment with Light. Much as I enjoy my daily lessons, you will agree that it makes a great change from teaching Latin grammar and essay-writing in English. It is wonderful to have this other agenda with young adults soon about to leave for the world of tomorrow.

The Future: a personal view

Alex Wildwood

Experiment with Light can take some pride in the way it has grown and convinced many Friends of its value without setting itself up as one more Listed Informal Group within the Yearly Meeting.[1] But what of the future? At present Rex Ambler is still around to speak of how he discovered it and what its basis is; but if the Experiment lasts for another ten or twenty years, it's going to evolve, add some things and lose some things. How can we be sure it doesn't lose the baby with the bathwater?

It seems to me that we have to be faithful to what we need to do with it in this generation; if we get that right, it may well have a life beyond our age. But we should be careful not to set up a rigid structure—mainly to take care of the more distant future—because that's how we institutionalise something and kill its spirit. It is wiser to do what is effective now and let it continue to evolve, just as it has already done in its few years of existence. Different forms of wording for the Experiment have appeared because some people are more comfortable with a more traditional form of language, others with a more psychological approach. Some, like Kerstin Backman, have even adapted it to non-Quaker groups. If each development is discerned to be "in the Life", we can trust that it will embody the original vision even as it grows and changes in ways that we can't envisage or control.

But we still need to ask how much control or structure may be needed to keep the whole movement alive and true to its essence. My own bias is towards having a bit of structure, because without it we can lose the gem at the centre. There are elements which must remain clear and definite. If they're not clarified, the whole thing can dissipate in the very process of its expanding.

At the moment Experiment with Light only has its written and recorded materials and what might be a dwindling band of people with the

[1] [A group may be listed in Britain Yearly Meeting's annual Book of Meetings if its aims, purpose and manner of proceeding are consistent with Friends' testimonies and methods. It should be open to all Friends and Attenders, it should be properly constituted, and membership levels should indicate a continued interest within the Yearly Meeting. Most Light groups would not meet these criteria: some are not open to all; they do not have formal officers; some may be established for only a limited time and they do not have formal aims. *Editor*]

experience to go and introduce it to Meetings. I think this may not be enough. If you want something to catch fire, you have to bring it to a critical moment at which it can take off and continue under its own momentum. The first Quakers, we know, thought they would only be needed for a generation; by the end of that time they expected the entire church to have got the message so that they could disappear. The mission of the Valiant Sixty was a conscious attempt to reach the critical point.

But if you send out your Valiant Sixty, how do you get your "quality control"? How do you ensure that the people who go out and talk about the Experiment do know what they're talking about and transmit a version of it faithful to the spirit of what Rex Ambler has so valuably uncovered? Those of us who have been in any way involved in overseeing its growth to this point have heard of people who have not had very good experiences with the Experiment. That probably comes from how it was introduced, insufficient preparation as people open themselves to what may be revealed—and perhaps a lack of safeguards in the way it has spread.

Is it always made clear to participants that it's a spiritual process and not (primarily) a psychological one? How does a Light Group avoid merely becoming a poor kind of encounter group (which is how I've heard people describe the process of sharing after the period of expectant waiting)? How do we answer those who worry that it is dangerous because it can open up all kinds of issues for people? Does it need to be something done under the care of the Meeting as a whole, with the awareness of—and hopefully willing involvement of—elders and overseers? Might people come upon insights and emotions which they don't know how to handle—and what is the responsible way of allowing for this? Of course, the fundamental question is do we really trust that it is God/Spirit guiding the process—as earlier Friends clearly did? Probably such problems arise when the group members don't follow the process through, as John Lampen suggests in his chapter. But who creates the safeguards and sees that they are observed?

I am not arguing for a controlling authority. Too often people seem to think that every structure is bound to be authoritarian and therefore a bad thing. But surely we have learnt since the 1960s that authority can lie in the work itself instead of in a hierarchy. By immersing yourself in an evolving tradition, by giving yourself to the service of it, *you* become the authority. As William Penn wrote of George Fox, "He exercised no authority but over evil, and that everywhere and in all, but with love, compassion and long-suffering".[2] Such authority does not grow in isolation, but by face to face encounters with others equally committing themselves to the same service and willing and able to honestly explore and examine their experiences together in complete equality of "rank".

The model I have in mind is the one found in the world of therapeutic trainings or the Quaker Alternatives to Violence Project, where you find peer accountability, support and training. The basis consists of the body of the work, the sum of group experiences, and the people who become practitioners of it in a mutual community of learning and sharing which safeguards the "standards" of the practice. I find this works very powerfully with no need for a top-down type of authority. If those people who take a process seriously and are moved by it communicate with one another as a group of equals, it will be enough. Of course, some of them can opt out, or follow individual paths as trainers, and we can't stop them. It is probably a good thing that we don't ask for that degree of control. The Alternatives to Violence Project manuals spell out their guidelines; if someone has completed the training and follows these, their work can be called "AVP". If they move away from them, good luck to them, but they shouldn't use the AVP name to describe what they are doing.

Paradoxically this demands a degree of organisation, because people do want to be in touch with one another. They need to feel they are part of a community which comes together to learn things; they get a sense of where the others are coming from and can validate (or question) one another's work. And this has to be arranged, maybe in the form of an annual gathering, like the Tutors' Development weekend at Woodbrooke. It would be a space where people could say to one another, "Look, this is coming up. For us it's a completely new situation, Have you met it? How did you deal with it?" I think that could be really valuable. The work needs to move outwards and deepen as it does so, but it needs to be brought back to the peer group in this way for regular re-evaluation. This is the way to revive enthusiasm and commitment and a means of replenishing the pool of Friends able to introduce the Experiment to our Meetings.

It may also be the place to experiment with variations on the theme, such as trying alternative wordings. This does happen in the Light Groups themselves, but without any forum for feedback which would bring promising developments back into the whole system. I feel that an early weakness of Experiment with Light was that it was heavily dependent on

[2] *The Journal of George Fox* (ed. John Nickalls, Religious Society of Friends, 1975) page xliv.

Rex Ambler's original set of prompts, which did not suit all conditions of Friends, as Diana Lampen explains in her chapter. One task of such a gathering might be to consider all the alternatives that have so far been tried, as well as new ideas. Is the choice a simple matter of preference, or are there deeper issues? Should we try to write more sets of prompts for different situations, as Rex did with his *Meditation on the Group*, and *Meditation on the World*? Should we look still wider and try to imagine what, say, a Buddhist set might look like?

This is very different from a "membership organisation", a development which could well be fatal. There have been several movements which sought to revitalise British Quakerism in recent years, and many of them ended up as minority "special interest groups" within the Yearly Meeting. They stopped having a wider influence, and in a few cases the outcome became a feeling of "them and us". One has to be really vigilant to avoid that kind of exclusivity. For the Experiment to avoid becoming an off-putting clique it must be transparent about the process itself and in general be willing to welcome people into individual Light Groups, whilst being really clear about when a group needs to be "closed" for reasons of building trust, safety and confidence. How can existing groups help newcomers form new groups? Can we be vigilant about involving newcomers in the practice even if they cannot be admitted to a particular group?

The mission of Experiment with Light is to offer a process to Friends which they can use for discernment and spiritual growth. It does not try to tell Friends what to think about things. There is a lot of writing and discussion in western religion about what one should think and believe, but far less about actual spiritual practices. (There is a huge hunger for such practices today but a lot of it is being expressed outside the organised structures of religion). Even amongst Friends—certainly in Britain—we have failed to teach people practices central to Quaker spirituality (such as Clearness Meetings, or how to "centre down"). The Experiment does have its rationale for why we do things in a certain way, which is profoundly based upon Quaker Christian insights, but essentially it is the teaching of a practice. I think that makes a world of difference, and to return to an earlier point, such structure and organisation as we need must focus on the promotion and spreading of this practice—which is, in essence, really something very simple and accessible.

I think Experiment with Light can be a leaven in our Yearly Meeting today. I equate it with things like Clearness Meetings, as an essential and inherently Quaker process which could be useful to any kind of groups but has a vital role amongst Friends. It can kindle a specifically Quaker understanding—based on a sense of a "listening spirituality" of how we can be led, both individually and in a group. It is a place where we can learn to wait, really wait, and listen to our lives. I don't see it as "problem-solving" and I prefer it when the prompts ask very broad questions, like (at the very beginning, after centring ourselves, "What do I need to be aware of at the moment?" Then the process follows from whatever answer we receive to that. This spaciousness, together with a deep sense that we will be led as the Light unfolds within us, really would be leaven for our Society today if more Friends were practising it.

Earlier generations of Friends had their public Meetings and their retired Meetings, but they also had a wealth of spiritual practice during the week, including regular bible reading and prayer, which I suspect few of us share in the twenty-first century. So it is a good and healthy discipline to have a new form of practice where a group of us gather together between one Sunday and the next. And of course Experiment with Light can be an individual practice too.

Indeed, if the kind of structure I am advocating does form itself, I would like to see it reaching out to all the Area Meetings and telling them what Experiment with Light has to offer Friends. Harvey Gilman said of outreach that it is about letting people know that we're here, and who we are. That's all that is needed. It is the same with this; surely we need to make Experiment with Light available and known, and say that there are people experienced and skilful in introducing it, who are accountable to one another. A range of opportunities could be offered, from a talk with a small experiential component up to a full introduction to the process over a weekend.

In 2001 I wrote, *Paradoxically, in the midst of the sense of urgency and activism that the state of our world elicits, there is a great need for expectant waiting, for not seeking to act "by our own strength", as early Friends would say. As the world around us speeds us in the death-throes of a bankrupt society, we need to be encouraging a greater sinking down in our gathered Meetings; we need to be more diligent in waiting, listening, discerning the call—to really know where we are led.*[3] I think Experiment with Light can have a crucial part to play in this.

[3] Alex Wildwood: "Tradition and Transition" *Woodbrooke Journal, Winter 2001*

Researching Experiment with Light

Helen Meads

The research

In 2003 I started researching the Experiment for an academic degree. I talked to Diana and John Lampen, then Rex Ambler, who had invited someone to undertake the work. I interviewed 21 Experimenters over a six month period, undertook "participant observation" in a newly formed Light group over a 15 month period and subsequently in other groups, some one-off. I was invited to participate in the November 2004 Glenthorne Experiment with Light retreat, which was intended for those most closely involved in disseminating the practice to determine what direction to take. Most of what my informants said was recorded on minidisc. I also talked to whoever would talk to me about anything to do with the Experiment. Most of my informants Experimented in Light groups, but a few did not.

There are no statistics of the numbers of Light groups, nor Experimenters, and I did not try to collate any; my research was qualitative, not quantitative. How widespread the practice is varies from year to year as groups fold and new ones begin. In 2002 Rex claimed there were between fifty and sixty groups worldwide.[1] I would estimate that there were between twenty and thirty groups active in Britain during the period of my fieldwork.

As I began my research one Friend told me that what happened to Experimenters was so dear to them she thought I would find it difficult to get them to share their experiences with me. It transpired she had been hurt by others' careless comments when she had entrusted her own. In the event, Friends did share their experiences of the Light openly with me and I felt very privileged both to be able to listen and to be present when some of the most difficult and the most wonderful things happened.

I then spent four years thinking about what Experimenters had told me, poring over it, listening to it, transcribing it, reading it, reading other material (some of it Quaker), theorising about it and writing it. Some things became clear only as I wrote, reviewed, edited and re-edited. I began to wonder whether those Experimenters would recognise their own experience or agree with what I was saying; some of them told me they did and no one said they didn't.

At one point I was challenged by Friends who did not Experiment. They suggested I was asserting that Experimenters' experience was somehow

[1] Rex Ambler: *Light to Live By* (Quaker Books, 2004) p.60

more spiritual than that of those who worked steadily away in Quaker committees where the spiritual experience was reflective and directed to the work itself, rather than personal and dramatic. I think this is one of the reasons Experimenters are reluctant to talk of their experiences, except in their own Light groups where there is a common understanding arising from the shared experience: they do not want to be misunderstood, to be thought to be claiming to be special, so they keep quiet.

What I found in the research

Clearly in writing up my research and summarising it in this chapter I have picked out the most obvious experiences. This might give the impression that everyone I spoke to or observed had such experiences or were changed as I describe and that, if this doesn't happen to you, you're doing something "wrong". This is not so. As was also my personal experience from time to time, Friends seemed also to experience nothing in their Experiments. One interviewee said to me, though, "Even when nothing's happened, something's happened" and I believe he is right. Sometimes we just don't identify at the time what has happened and sometimes the "nothing" is the message. In my own case, for example, when I had a spell of falling asleep in Experiments, eventually it dawned on me that the message was that I was stretching myself too far, doing too much and needed more rest. It still happens now sometimes.

Experimenters told me they came to find truths about themselves and their relationships; they found what got in the way of their living their lives as honestly as they would like or being fully at ease with themselves and others. Their Experimenting led to different ways of being, conducting their relationships and experiencing the world. They spoke variously of becoming vegetarian; being unable to tell white lies for social convenience; one silently weeping at a pain she could not share except to say that she knew she had to accept the way things were; another ceasing to struggle with one daughter's twenty year refusal to speak to another daughter; letting go of toxic anger; being able to retire; giving up long-held Quaker jobs; discerning the true nature of feelings for family; facing past violent acts; accepting that occupational stress was something to rise above; beginning to understand what underlay an obsession with sex. None of this was comfortable or easy for any of them.

Some of these realisations came from the most unlikely Friends: one of the incidents of violence was told by a Friend well known for promoting the peace testimony; another revealed potential mistakes he had made in life-or-death decisions, saying: "I need to forgive myself." To share these risked loss of reputation (or more), exposed their vulnerabilities to others as it was newly exposed to themselves, and expressed great trust in fellow

Experimenters. When they shared with each other in depth, their relationships changed and the combination of Experimenting together and then sharing amplified the experience, not least because they would then carry around others' images as well as their own. They also carried their fellow-Experimenters' sharing including these images under the protocol of confidentiality, as they knew their fellow-Experimenters might do with the knowledge of their own sharing. The protocol served to bind them still closer and increased the intimacy.

What Experimenters had in common also went beyond uncomfortably facing themselves, to more transcendent experiences. On one occasion, two Experimenters shared the same image, of a pool of water and its significance, of peace. Another said: "I had an image of Experiment with Light as a mountain spring, and in the biblical sense of the water of life, which when you drink it, you don't get thirsty any more." One described her Experimenting as "an experience of relating to something beyond me that was illuminating me, so that there was a separate entity which was very real, very alive" then later as "a dynamic going on between something beyond me but also in me" and as bringing her into "right relationship with God." Another wrote a poem exploring her transportation in the meditation through all five senses. One described strange shifting scenarios he did not himself understand. Another began the long process of coming to terms with severe physical and emotional pain. More than one talked of feeling a very deep sense of peace, tapping into and being guided by a force or energy, an inner spiritual resource, infinite potential, "external intentionality"; some named it as "the Light", outside or other than themselves, yet part of themselves, both immanent and transcendent.

Friends also noted a magnification of their spiritual experience in their Experimenting in Light groups, so they were aware that their experience was deepened and reinforced by their sharing: Experimenting led to their listening more, paying more attention to spiritual matters and deepening both daily spiritual practice and experience in Meeting for Worship. This sharing is radically different from the rest of British Quaker behaviour, where Friends do not talk to each other of their unbidden mystical experiences and there is no structured opportunity to talk about what may have been happening to them in the silence of Meeting for Worship.

As I write this, I'm still in the process of thinking about what should go into my thesis and what there is to say about what the Experiment really is and how it fits into the ordinary run of British Quaker life. One thing I can say, however, is that it seems clear to me that 21st century Experimenters with Light (although they do not specifically seek "convincement" or encounter with God, because they do not want to assume that God will come when called) do go through a process of meeting God which is very like that of the earliest Friends in the 17th century.

Discernable stages were apparent in the process Experimenters underwent over a length of time (and these correspond to those identified for early Friends[2]):

1 realisation of Truth (God breaks in);
2 not in right relationship, feeling darkness (conviction of sin);
3 possibility of changed behaviour (choice of repentance);
4 coming into right relationship (born again into perfection);
5 intimacy within the group (gathering together);
6 acceptance (mission).

The 21st century is a much more complex world than the 17th, though. Early Friends' experience led them to a final stage of spreading the word, undergoing mission in an attempt to change what, in the light of their experience, they found unacceptable. Experimenters' final stage, however, is acceptance of what they feel they cannot change. More than this, Experimenters keep quiet about their experience, even with other Friends unless those Friends are Experimenters.

There is a dichotomy and tension between the Experiment's inherent dynamic of being led by the Light and the need to organise in order to spread the practice. Both the 1998 and the 2004 Glenthorne retreats decided that there should be no Listed Informal Group for the Experiment, since that would be to sideline it and potentially prevent its permeating the whole of Britain Yearly Meeting. [3] But without any formal organisation how was it to become more widespread? In using the Experiment to try to find the way forward, Friends were given beautiful images of butterflies, earthen vessels, candles, a petrie dish of magenta liquid, but little that was practical—so very different from early Friends.

Being a researcher

I cannot divorce my own experience as researcher from the subject of researching the Experiment, because I am convinced that to research the Experiment and find out anything meaningful about it, one must also do one's utmost to live Experimentally and be Truthful.[4]

[2] See the analysis of a passage of Howgill in Ben Pink Dandelion: *Convinced Quakerism*. (Southeastern Yearly Meeting, USA, 2003) pp. 11-12.

[3] [See footnote on page 84. *Editor*.]

[4] I have written about this in more detail elsewhere: Helen Meads: "Insider Research into 'Experiment with Light': Uncomfortable Reflexivity in a Different Field." *Quaker Studies* 11, no. 2 (2007), pp. 282-298.

My experience was that the research and my spiritual life became inextricably intertwined and this intertwining intensified as the work progressed. This was very challenging and uncomfortable personally. I found myself making or experiencing very fundamental changes in my own life: a fifteen year relationship ended; my sexual orientation changed; my appearance changed completely; I became more open; I began to understand and come to terms with my family influences; I became entrepreneurial and I began to see everything differently. I can't pretend that I did this on my own; I had an enormous amount of help from a wide range of friends unconnected with the Experiment.

In an Experiment in 2003 I had my first real knowing-in-a-whole-way encounter with the reality of the Divine. What had been a notion, an idea I understood intellectually, and was aware had been others' experience, became my own experience. It was only in a later Experiment in 2007, at the same time as I was finalising this chapter, that I became aware of how significant this had been in the way I had understood what my informants were telling me.

The point about the Experiment is that one understands truths about oneself, one's relationships and the world in a total, whole way, not as a "head", "rational" or logical matter. I was advised at one point that I needed to give up Experimenting while I wrote up my thesis, but I wasn't prepared to do that, for good methodological reasons[5] as well as personal ones. One dear friend, not a Quaker, said to me at one very difficult point, when I very nearly gave up the PhD, that universities were established separately from the church for a very good reason. I was trying to break down that separation whilst being true to both the academic and the spiritual; it was a struggle. If I hadn't carried on trying, there would have been no purpose to the work. The Experiment demanded this of me; I was called.

The questions I'm left with

My main remaining puzzle is why the Experiment has not been more widely embraced by British Quakers. It is practised by only a few and by no means in every Meeting. In Diana's chapter she points out the need for Experimenters to communicate with their Meetings to avoid divisions, but what of Meetings' responsibilities to their small groups? What are Friends wary of? We are corporately enjoined to think it possible we may be

[5] "Uncomfortable reflexivity" means that the researcher has to struggle with her identity, in my case my religious identity, and to give up Experimenting while writing up my work would have been to put aside part of my identity, which would have meant being untrue to the challenge of the method I was using.

mistaken and to live adventurously,[6] yet a practice which offers these very prospects is sometimes looked at askance and sometimes even treated with hostility. Why do all Friends not welcome the mystical experiences that only some may have? One Experimenter told me that he thought that plain speaking had become something of a shibboleth. Or possibly we have not until now, with this book, communicated widely and effectively enough what Experimenters' experiences are.

Ben Pink Dandelion discussed British Friends' "Culture of Silence" in relation to belief,[7] but British Friends have also been silent about individual spiritual experience, and not just experiences in the Experiment. Perhaps Experimenters have been reluctant to talk about these experiences because they have been wary of other Friends' reactions, fearing that they might be accused of claiming to be somehow special when they know they are not.

It could be that there is a tension not just between Experimenters' spiritual experiences and the need to organise, but also more generally between spiritual experience and the principles behind Quaker business structures. This may relate to the difference between whole ways of knowing (sudden and complete body, mind, heart and spirit awareness) and rational, logical ways; perhaps it is so strongly held in British Friends' corporate culture that the discernment of the group is more valid than the individual's, especially where the individual's experience is radical spiritually. Maybe British Friends have such a strong corporate memory of the James Nayler incident that they still fear the emergence of a maverick group and so constrain individual leadings too tightly. Possibly that is why Monthly Meetings did not respond to the epistle[8] sent to them by Experimenters gathered at Glenthorne in 2004.

Why, too, do we still lack the fire of early Friends, the very point which first sent Rex off on his studies?[9] Why do we prefer acceptance to mission, even after deep experience of the Light? Is it to do with the times and the society we live in? Is it because our experience is not as dramatic, because we experience a more general Light, not the Light of a living Christ? Or is it because we are defeatist, or are we, as we might prefer to say, realistic in the face of apathy? Are we too liberal, too uncertain, actually, after all, unconvinced?

[6] *Quaker Faith & Practice: The Book of Christian Discipline of the Yearly Meeting of the Religious Society of Friends (Quakers) in Britain.* (The Yearly Meeting of the Religious Society of Friends (Quakers) in Britain, 1995) 1.02.17 & 1.02.27.

[7] Ben Pink Dandelion: *A Sociological Analysis of the Theology of Quakers: The Silent Revolution.* (Edwin Mellen Press, 1996) pp. 238-250.

[8] See page 15 above.

[9] Rex Ambler: *Light to Live By*, p.2

Experiences in the Light

Isaac Penington

Some of the most moving and authentic accounts of living in the Light come from the writings of Isaac Penington (1616—1679). In various writings he offered some "advices and answers" to those who doubted the truth of the heart to which he witnessed.

Now, after many a weary step and deep sickness of heart, when we were come even near to despair of ever finding and enjoying what our souls so sorely longed after, it pleased the Lord at length in his tender mercy to appear among us, and by the directions of his Holy Spirit to turn our minds inwards; showing us, that *that* which we sought without, was to be found within: telling us, that there was the kingdom, which was not to be found by observations without, but by meeting with, and subjecting to, the light and power of life within. And when we were solicitous how to know it from the darkness and deceit within, this answer was given us from the Lord; Its nature will discover itself; it will find out and reprove whatever is reprovable, and furnish the soul with strength against [that]. Oh, blessed sound from the Lord God of life, who thus drew our hearts to wait upon him; and showed us how to wait, and what to wait for, and where we might meet with that which our hearts so exceedingly desired and panted after! And truly as our minds were thus turned inwards, the holy light did shine upon us…[1]

A man cannot pray when he will; but he is to watch and to wait, when the Father will kindle in him living breathings towards himself. So the word of God (whether of exhortation or instruction) is a gift, which is to be waited for, and then to be given forth in the life and strength of that Spirit which caused it to spring. Indeed it is a hard matter either to speak the word of the Lord, or to hear the word of the Lord. A man may easily speak what he invents, and another may easily hear and judge of such words; but to speak the word of life, requires the tongue of [those who are] learned in the language of God's Spirit; and to hear the word of life, requires a quickened ear.[2]

Christ is known, received and obeyed as a seed; as the seed of life, as the seed of the kingdom, as [yeast], as salt; as a little small thing rising up in the

[1] *Life and Immortality Brought to Life by the Gospel* in *The Works* vol.iv, p.160 [Square brackets indicate editorial alterations.]

[2] *Concerning the Worship of the Living God* in *The Works* vol.ii, p.212

heart against all that is great and mighty… The soul being in darkness, sin and death, this appears as a light to [reveal all these] and to lead out of darkness… into the redeeming power. And then, to them that thus receive it and wait… in the fear and humility which it gives… it appears as life quickening the soul, and as power enabling it in some measure to live to God…[3]

And ye that would not be deceived, sink deep beneath the thoughts, reasonings, and consultations of the earthly mind, that ye may meet with somewhat of the kingdom and power (which carries its own evidence and demonstration with it), and may be gathered into it, and find a sense, knowledge, and judgment there, which never was deceived, nor can deceive… It came from the light of the Father. It lives in the light of the Father. It sees in that light; yea, there its judgment and understanding is, where deceit never had power to enter. But he that… judges as a man, concerning the things of God, by what he can gather out of the Scriptures, or conclude from his own sense, knowledge, and experience, he may easily err; yea, indeed, he is in the way of error in so doing. For the pure religion, the pure knowledge, the right judgment, the living faith, begin in the power and demonstration of the Spirit; and these are… out of the compass of [human] comprehension. And he that passeth not these bounds never meets with the life, power, and virtue of truth. He may meet with a body of notions and formed knowledge, wherein he may tell of the fall of man and restoration by Christ, and very exactly, according to a literal description; but the life, the true knowledge, the powerful virtue, is another thing, and is met with in another country, whither man cannot travel, but [when] he is stripped of himself, and new formed, made and brought forth in another.[4]

But how may men know that these are true commands of the Lord, and not imaginations or opinions of their own? When the principle of life is known and that which God hath begotten [is] felt in the heart, the distinction between what God opens and requires there and what springs up in man's wisdom, reason and imagination, is very manifest.[5]

How may a man come to the power of the endless life? By waiting to feel it. There is somewhat of God near every man; which, [if he allow] his spirit to retire and wait on the Lord, the Lord will give him to feel in the seasons

[3] *Some things of great Weight and Concernment to all* (1667) in *The Works* vol.iii, p.9

[4] *Truth Revived out of the Apostacy* in *The Works* vol.iv p.13

[5] *Some Questions and Answers shewing Mankind his Duty* in *The Works* vol.ii, p.276

of his good pleasure. For it is near man, not as a talent always to lie dead and buried, but to work in him, and bring him out of his own sinful, corrupt nature into his holy, pure nature.

[Each of us] may feel and know the power of this life by its nature, properties, manner and end of working in the heart. It enlightens the soul, it quickens to God, it draws the heart from that which is manifestly and sensibly evil without dispute, it opens the eye to see and discern that which is holy and good, inflaming the mind with desires after it. Now, this is the appearance of the Holy One, who thus appears and begins to work…[6]

Now the Lord knows, these things I do not utter in a boasting way; but would rather be speaking of my nothingness, my emptiness, my weakness, my manifold infirmities, which I feel more than ever… But I can not but utter to the praise of my God, and I feel his arm stretched out for me; and my weakness which I feel in myself, is not my loss, but advantage before him.[7]

[6] *Truth Revived out of the Apostacy* in *The Works* vol.iv p.37

[7] *The Testimony of Thomas Ellwood concerning Isaac Penington* in Isaac Penington: *The Works* (Quaker Heritage Press 1994-7) vol.i p.8ff.

Appendix: Meditation Guides for Workshops and Light Groups

The meditations are based on the practice of early Friends, as indicated in the epistles of George Fox and writings of Isaac Penington, and discussed in Rex Ambler's paper "The discipline of light" in *The Presence in the Midst* (Quaker Theology Seminar 1997). Each of the six steps should last about five to seven minutes: the words of each prompt should be read first, then followed by silence.

Experiment with Light is not a ritual, so the six prompts will never take on a final and unchangeable form. Several regular Light Groups as they grew used to the practice and to one another have experimented with different wordings, which they have often found very valuable. These all depend to some extent on the Group's knowledge of Rex Ambler's original version, or the words and thought of George Fox, just as in music a single theme can lead to many variations. The first three versions given below have been tested in different groups and found suitable for those learning the practice individually or on an introductory course. The first of them was devised by Rex and revised with help from Catherine King Ambler and Helen Meads. The second, by Diana Lampen and Elizabeth Brown, is closer to early Friends' practice, while the third, created by Klaus Huber for a workshop with Young Friends, uses extracts from *Truth of the Heart: an anthology of George Fox* (Quaker Books, 2001). The fourth suggestion is offered particularly to some evangelical Friends who asked for the meditation to be related to the Bible.

I. *Revised version of the original meditation for the individual.*

1. **Relax body and mind**. Make yourself comfortable. Feel the weight of your body on the chair (or the floor). Let all the tension go, in each part of your body. Let your immediate worries go, your current preoccupations. Be relaxed, but alert. Let yourself become wholly receptive. **(Pause)**

2. In this receptive state of mind, let **the real concerns of your life** emerge. Ask yourself, "What is really going on in my life?", but do not try to answer the question. Let the answer come. You can be specific: "What is happening in my relationships, my work, my Meeting, in my own heart and mind?" And more specifically still: "Is there anything here that makes me feel uncomfortable, uneasy?" As we gradually become aware of these things we are beginning to experience the light. **(Pause)**

3. Now **focus on one issue** that presents itself, one thing that gives you a sense of unease. Try to get a sense of this thing as a whole. Deep down you know what it is all about, but you don't normally allow yourself to take it all in and absorb the reality of it. Now is the time to do so. You don't have to get involved in it again, or get entangled with the feelings around it. Keep a little distance, so that you can see it clearly. Let the light show you what is really going on here. 'What is it about this thing', you can ask, 'that makes me feel uncomfortable?' Let the answer come. And when it

does, let a word or image also come that says what it's really like, this thing that concerns me. **(Pause)**

4. Now ask yourself **what makes it like that.** Don't try to explain it. Just wait in the light till you can see what it is. Let the full truth reveal itself, or as much truth as you are able to take at this moment. The answer will come. **(Pause)**

5. When the answer comes **welcome it.** It may be painful or difficult to believe with your normal conscious mind, but if it is the truth you will recognize it immediately. You will realise that it is something that you need to know. Trust the light. Say yes to it. It will show you new possibilities. It will show you the way through. So however the news seems to be at first, accept it and let its truth pervade your whole being. **(Pause)**

6. As soon as you accept what is being revealed to you, you will begin to **feel different**. Accepting truth about yourself is like making peace. Something is being resolved. If none of this seems to have happened, do not worry. It may take longer. Notice how far you have got this time and pick it up on another occasion. In any case this is a process we do well to go through again and again, so that we can continue to grow and become more like the people we are meant to be. **(Pause)** When you feel ready, open your eyes, stretch your limbs, and bring the meditation to an end.

II. *A version using fewer words, based on early Friends' practice.*

1. **Be still.** Sit comfortably. Breath slowly several times. Relax and let your mind become quiet. Be still. **(Pause)**

2. Wait. Be receptive. Turn to the Light. **(Pause)**

3. Allow the Light to show you your real concerns. (Pause)

4. **Be cool.** Keep a little distance as you focus on something which is significant for you. Let the Light show you what is really happening there. If feelings or questions arise, hold them in the Light. Wait for clarity. **(Pause)**

5. Open yourself to what is being shown. Wait, and trust the Light. Let the understanding come. **(Pause)**

6. **Submit to what you are shown.** Accept it and welcome it. Continue to wait in the Light. Be open to new possibilities. Be thankful for your experience, whatever it has been. **(Pause)** When you feel ready, open your eyes, stretch your limbs, and bring the meditation to an end.

III. *A practice using the words of George Fox.*

1. Keep within. For the Measure is within, and the Light is within, and the Pearl is within you. **(Pause)**

2. Let the Light that shines in every one of your consciences search you thoroughly, and it will let you clearly see. As the Light opens and exercises your conscience, it will let you see invisible things, which are clearly seen by that which is invisible in you. **(Pause)**

3. As the Light appeared, all appeared that is out of the Light—darkness, death, temptations, the unrighteous, the ungodly; all was manifest and seen in the Light. **(Pause)**

4. Do not look at the temptations, confusions, corruptions, but at the Light that discovers them. For looking down at corruption and distraction, you are swallowed up in it; but looking at the Light that discovers them, you will see over them. There is the first step to peace. **(Pause)**

5. The Light will lead you out of darkness into the light of life, into the way of peace and into the life and power of Truth. **(Pause)**

6. Living in the Truth ye live in the love and unity. In the Light walk, and ye will shine. **(Pause)** When you feel ready, open your eyes, stretch your limbs, and bring the meditation to an end.

IV *A suggested set of prompts drawn from the Bible.*

1. The Lord is good to everyone who trusts in him, so it is best for us to wait in patience—to wait for him to save us. [Lamentations 3:25-26]
or "Be still and know that I am God." [Psalm 46:10]

2. "Come to me, all whose work is hard, whose load is heavy; and I will give you relief." [Matthew 11:28]

3. The Lord answered her: "Martha, Martha! You are worried and troubled over so many things, but just one is needed." [Luke 10:41-42]

4. "I will lead my blind people by roads they have never travelled. I will turn their darkness into light and make rough country smooth before them." [Isaiah 42:16]

5. "Peace is my parting gift to you, my own peace, such as the world cannot give. Set your troubled hearts at rest, and banish your fears." [John 14:27]

6. Thy instruction is wonderful; therefore I gladly keep it. Thy word is revealed and all is light. [Psalm 119: 129-130]

Printed resources

Rex Ambler: *Truth of the Heart: an anthology of George Fox* (Quaker Books, 2001, reprinted 2007)

This collection of passages from the writings of George Fox (1624-1691) is meant to do two things: to make available his clearest and most profound writings from the whole range of his works and to display them in such a way as to show the connections between them. Each is presented in its original words with a modern paraphrase. By reading the text through one gains a picture of Fox's whole vision.

Rex Ambler: *Light To Live By: An Exploration In Quaker Spirituality* (Quaker Books, 2002, reprinted 2009)

This book is a companion volume to *Truth of the Heart: An Anthology of George Fox*. The author describes a "personal practice of meditation which I discovered in early Friends" and tells "the story of my attempts to use the practice and develop it in my own personal life." Rex Ambler sees Fox, in a tract of 1653, clearly describing a meditative process about which he goes into in detail, relating it to his own personal exploration and development. In the appendix he outlines the stages of meditation, based on the practice of early Friends but given present day relevance and made useable in a workshop format.

Work is in hand on papers about "Quaker Eldership and Experiment with Light" and "Starting a Light Group". Go to *www.experiment-with-light .org.uk* to check if these are ready, and how to obtain them.

Compact discs

CD 1. This contains two talks by Rex Ambler, given at Charney Manor in March 1998. The first talk is on the early Quaker experience, to be used with an enclosed leaflet. The second is an introduction to the practice.

CD 2. This contains two versions of the meditation used in the "experiment with Light", drawing on the insights of early Friends and the psychologist Eugene Gendlin. Each comprises six readings with silences in between. The first side contains fuller introductions to each section of the meditation for those who are new to it. The second side is more concise, for those who have already used the process several times.

Please note that Rex Ambler has asked that the above two items should normally be sold as a pair.

CD 3. This contains two further versions of the meditations. The first is a meditation on our relationships with others (this was formerly called "meditation on the Group"); the second is a meditation on the World.

Many people involved in the Experiment have found a natural progression from focusing on ourselves to looking outwards at the group we belong to and the wider world.

CD 4 (two-disc set). This contains an alternative form of meditation, leading through the same process but based more closely on George Fox's own words. This is supplemented by readings from Truth of the Heart, Rex Ambler's selection and translation of passages from George Fox's writings which illuminate the Experiment with Light process. This CD also contains an additional "wordless" meditation for those very familiar with the practice, in which the stages are marked only by the sound of a bell.

CD 5. This version of the meditation is intended for those who have already used the process a number of times. Like Tape 4 it uses some of George Fox's words taken from Rex Ambler's selection and translation, *Truth of the Heart*, (Quaker Books, 2001) . The references are: part 1, sections 23, 82, 74, 75, 91 and 128; and part 2, sections 79 and 66.

This is followed by another version of this meditation using the briefest of prompts for those who want as few words as possible.

In 2010, each CD costs £4.50 including the 2-disc set CD4. This price includes post and packing. (It may need to be increased in future.) Audiotapes are no longer generally available, but if it is important to you to have the meditations on tape, please consult Diana Lampen at lampen@hopeproject.co.uk

In Britain and Europe: please order CDs from: The Quaker Bookshop, Friends House, Euston Road, London NW1 2BJ. They are also available over the counter at The Quaker Centre in Friends House, London.

In USA and Canada: Contact Quaker Books of Friends General Conference, 1216 Arch St. #2B, Philadelphia, PA 19107, USA 800-966-4556 (9 AM-4:30 PM EST); or online from Quaker Books of Friends General Conference www.quakerbooks.org/experiment_with_light.php

The Internet

Experiment with Light has a website at *www.experiment-with-light.org.uk* It lists resources and coming events. It has printable files of most versions of the practice/meditation. It also contains some spoken files which can be downloaded, used and distributed free of charge, as there is no copyright on these materials. At the time of printing these include: the 1998 talks by Rex Ambler, from CD1; the practices on CDs 2 and 4, except the "wordless" version; and the readings from *Truth of the Heart*, also contained on CD4. Further additions and updates will be made from time to time.

Notes on the contributors

Rex Ambler taught theology at Birmingham University and, now retired, writes about Quaker theology and spirituality and runs workshops on Quaker practice. He describes in *Light to Live by* how the study of George Fox's writings led him to the development of Experiment with Light.

Kerstin Backman was born of Quaker parents in 1943 and joined the Society of Friends herself in 1971. She is a teacher of English, French and Latin at an upper secondary school in the Stockholm area. She is and has been active among Swedish Friends, among other things in the Faith and Practice committee, which has recently completed Sweden's first book of Faith and Practice.

John Daly writes: "I suffered from undiagnosed depression for most of my first fifty years. A combination of counselling and medication has now freed me from this burden. I trained as a scientist and have spent some years on research in marine biology and entomology. In the gaps I have spent twenty years in non-profit-making organic smallholding. I now aspire to be a poet."

John Gray was brought up as a Quaker, and **Bronwen** became a member in 1993. They are part of a Light Group which began in 1999 and which still meets monthly. They live with their two children in York, England; Bronwen and the children worship at Friargate Meeting.

Anne Hosking has worshipped with Friends all her adult life, in this Yearly Meeting and when living abroad. She was one of the founders of the Quaker Retreat Group, represented Quakers in the Retreat Association, was involved in spiritual direction and for a period led retreats and Experiments among Friends. She has shared in a regular, co-operative retreat with two others, and been active in Quaker Quest, the outreach project that began in north London. She values the meetings for worship with Questers as some of the deepest, most nourishing she has known.

Cynthia Jones wrote this reflection during a Light Group meeting about eight months after she joined Green Street Meeting in Philadelphia. She had previous experience with Quakerism through Green Street School and George School, two Quaker schools that her daughter attended. She says "I was already a Quaker before I was a Quaker." She uses these words to describe herself: "African American woman from New York City," "creative arts therapist," and "adventurer."

Diana Lampen is a teacher of yoga and pranayama who has introduced Experiment with Light to many Quaker meetings. She has been involved in peace work and conflict resolution in the U.K. and abroad for many years.

John Lampen teaches the creative handling of conflict in Britain and overseas. He has written *Mending Hurts* and *Twenty Questions about Jesus* for Friends, *The Peace Kit* for children, and he helped Brian Phillips to edit *Endeavours to Mend: Perspectives on British Quaker work in the world today.*

Marcelle Martin, a member of Chestnut Hill Meeting in Philadelphia Yearly Meeting, is the resident Quaker Studies teacher at Pendle Hill. She is the author of the Pendle Hill pamphlets, *Invitation to a Deeper Communion* and *Holding One Another in the Light.*

Judy Maurer was born in a little town in the mountains of Arizona, where her father was the Episcopalian minister. She began attending Friends' meetings during high school in New England and college in the Midwest (U.S.). She is director of development for Abuse Recovery Ministry & Services. Her husband Johan and she are shortly leaving for their ministry in Russia.

Helen Meads attended Meeting for Worship in Birmingham from 1979 until early 1981, then after a seventeen year gap she became a member in Yorkshire at High Flatts Quaker Meeting in 1998. She first learned of the Experiment when Rex Ambler spoke at a specially arranged Yorkshire General Meeting on 30 June 1999 and she has been a member of High Flatts Light group since it began in 2000. She has been a part-time postgraduate student at the University of Birmingham through the Centre for Postgraduate Quaker Studies at Woodbrooke since 2002 and hopes to submit her PhD thesis about Experiment with Light in 2008. She is a partner in Yorkshire Quaker Arts Projects, which in 2007 produced a film, "Go Inside to Greet the Light", about the Quaker resonances in James Turrell's Deer Shelter Skyspace.

Linda Panetta (pictures, page 73) is a photojournalist and founder of School of Americas Watch/NE (www.soawne.org), a grassroots human rights organization that seeks to close a military combat training school through nonviolent protests, media exposure and legislative work. She lectures extensively using her slides to educate others about the implications of U.S. foreign policy and the realities of war. She is also involved in a program supporting survivors of torture and their families. Her photographs can be viewed at: www.opticalrealities.org

Helene Pollock works as Director of Quaker Affairs at Haverford College in Haverford, PA. She is a member of Central Philadelphia Monthly Meeting. She has a particular interest in finding ways to help current-day Friends to relate to the spirituality of early Friends, and thus experience spiritual renewal for themselves.

Shelagh Robinson is a practicing psychotherapist. As a member of Quaker Life Central Committee she gives support to Local Meetings facing difficulties.

Nancy Saunders is a certified Focusing Oriented Therapist and psychologist, and a member of Swarthmore Monthly Meeting, Pennsylvania, where she serves as Clerk of the Meeting.

Alex Wildwood gave the 1999 Swarthmore Lecture and continues to explore the implications of different contemporary "movements of the spirit" for Friends today.